GW00705961

fat
free
forever!

Dianne Wilson's experience as a fashion
model, personal trainer and body shaping
expert have helped her to develop this body
shaping lifestyle to recover her shape after
giving birth to her twin sons.

The cover of this book is a photograph
of Dianne taken after she successfully lost
40 kilos, following the *Fat Free Forever!*
body shaping lifestyle.

Dianne and family.

fat free forever!

The Body Shaping Lifestyle

Dianne Wilson

RANDOM HOUSE AUSTRALIA

Random House Australia Pty Ltd
20 Alfred Street, Milsons Point, NSW 2061
http://www.randomhouse.com.au

First published by Mandarin 1996
First published by Random House Australia 1997
Reprinted 1998 (three times); 1999; 2001
This Random House Australia edition first published 2002

Typeset in Sabon by Asset Typesetting Pty Ltd and Midland Typesetters
Printed in China
Organised through Phoenix Offset

National Library of Australia
Cataloguing-in-publication Entry:
    Wilson, Dianne Barker.
    Fat free forever.
    [Rev. ed.]
    ISBN 1 74051 130 1
    1. Reducing diets. 2. Reducing exercises. 3. Low-fat diet.
    4. Weight loss. 5. Physical fitness. I. Title.
    613.25

The author and the publisher of this book are not medically trained and are not licensed to
give medical advice. Always consult your doctor before embarking on any weight loss
course. The facts provided are based on extensive research up until the publishing date;
however, the contents of products mentioned are subject to change by manufacturers from
time to time and those contents may vary from those listed in this book.

Although a useful guide when shopping, information in this book is not an endorse-
ment or recommendation of any product, manufacturers, companies or individuals.

The author and publisher of this book cannot take responsibility for any injuries
incurred by readers in performing any of the exercises outlined in this guide. As with any
program of exercise, it should be undertaken with care and with individuals working at
their own pace. Exercise guidelines have been provided to assist the reader. The author and
the publisher recommend that a sound base of knowledge be developed by the user prior
to embarking on any exercise program.

The author and publisher disclaim any liability, damage or loss whatsoever arising
directly or indirectly from the information contained in *Fat Free Forever*.

9 8 7 6 5 4 3 2 1

Foreword

Cardiovascular disease remains the largest single cause of death amongst Australians. This is true of many western countries. In addition, there are other large, often forgotten, non-lethal consequences such as time lost from work, hospitalisation, and long-term symptoms as a result of cardiovascular disease.

Fat Free Forever! is a very informative, easy to read and easy to follow piece of literature. It has great recipes sensibly listed under different food categories.

The book is enthusiastically written and I hope its readers will be contagiously affected by Dianne Wilson's optimistic style.

Finally, don't start changing things tomorrow – start now!

David W. Baron, FRACP
Cardiologist

St. Vincent's Hospital
Sydney, Australia

Dedication

To my beautiful boys Bentley and Beau. You are an answer to prayer! You are my world! I love you.

Contents

Stage 1

Lifestyle Principles

Stage 2

Food

Stage 3
Exercise

My Story

Life is full of choices.

If you eat fat, *you will* get fat.

If you overload on starchy carbohydrates (cereal, bread, potato, rice and pasta), *you will* get fat.

And if you starve yourself to be thin, *you will* get even fatter (eventually).

I have done the lot, and believe me – **it's true.**

•

From my mid-teens to early twenties, I went through the whole yoyo dieting thing, along with most of the other girls I knew. I would starve myself for a week just to fit into a pair of tiny jeans. I also suffered greatly when I had to eat in front of people. I was so nervous. One summer when I was away on holidays, I grazed on carrots and apples and drank only water for days on end. I certainly was the skinniest girl on the beach that summer.

> The greatest problem with not eating was
> that all I was doing was starving my muscle tissue
> and ruining my body shape.

Sure, I lost weight, but the less I ate, the more my poor body cried 'starvation', and clicked itself into a mode that was designed to store fat in times of 'famine' for protection. This made it nearly impossible to keep the fat off.

I have learned that people are either emotional eaters or emotional starvers. I was both – depending on the circumstances!

> Did you know that your body sometimes feels falsely
> comforted when it absorbs the fat you eat?

This is why emotional eaters usually head for the potato chips, buttered toast, peanut butter, hamburgers and chocolate. It takes a while for some people to realise that true comfort cannot come from a crinkle-cut anything. An instant 'high' soon converts to a long-term 'low'.

During all of this unintended craziness, though, I didn't know about or give a second thought to what this was doing to my body's metabolism.

When I was growing up, we always had skim milk and lots of fresh fruit in our house. We would arrive home each afternoon after school and Mum would hand my sister and me a carrot on our way through the front door. Lemonade was a special treat, as were chocolate biscuits.

It wasn't that Mum had us on a diet, it was because she was conscious of healthy eating, and it just grew on us.

I knew there was something important missing in all this healthy eating though, and that was the knowledge of how to put it all together. What we didn't know then but we do know now is that eating 'healthily' isn't necessarily going to give you the body shape of your dreams. A lot of health food is loaded with fats, and often the product – fish, for example – is great to start with, but when it's fried and served with chips for dinner, it's lethal!

I actually thought (along with thousands of other teenagers) that the only way to lose weight quickly was to just stop eating. My poor Mum. Can you imagine? What hope did she have trying to convince her teenage daughter *(who knew everything – of course)* not to do this to her body! But now I realise, with hindsight, that I had so many excellent alternatives.

1987 was a heavy year for this teenage girl. My father suffered terribly from heart problems – he had unstable angina and a 90% closure of his left ventricle. This was caused by heredity, smoking for more than 30 years, and long-term bad eating habits. My Grandma was a single mum of eleven kids during the Depression, as my Grandpa died when my Dad was just ten years old. This meant Grandma had to live on what you could call a tight budget. Fat came cheap!

It was hard for Dad to change his childhood eating habits. Even though Mum would prepare semi-healthy food, there would always be room for a few slices of bread and butter as well. Dad's weaknesses were chocolate and starchy carbohydrates. And if we had a roast dinner (like so many other families in Australia), it would be dripping in dripping.

What happened to my Dad shocked us all. It truly transformed our entire family's lifestyle for the better. My father survived major open-heart surgery and is alive and well today, more than 15 years down the track.

> Sitting by his bedside taught me something worthwhile: we can change our lives and the quality of them by making certain choices.

Mum spent hours, days and weeks, seeking out and modifying all kinds of new recipes and cooking methods. She even turned the Heart Foundation and Pritikin diet books upside-down – taking out the tablespoon of oil here and teaspoon of margarine there. Nothing was going to get in the way of reducing my Dad's cholesterol and weight. And, although she isn't a doctor, dietitian or even a personal trainer, she's smart and determined, and she did it!

Mum achieved amazing results from using no added fat. Not only did my father's cholesterol shrink to a very low level, but his body shape changed dramatically, and he had the energy and enthusiasm of a man at least ten years his junior. Dad's doctor, Sydney cardiologist Dr David Baron, was astounded at the short amount of time it took Mum to get Dad's cholesterol and weight down *before* his urgent heart operation.

Notice how I say Mum did a lot of the work. Dr Baron knew that with Dad's poor eating background he would need Mum to make the effort. Not everyone is as fortunate as my Dad, to have a 'personal chef' who is so good with fat free cooking and motivation. It is, however, *more than* possible for each person who reads this book to adopt a healthy motivational attitude that will allow them to set and achieve their very own healthy body shaping goals.

My entire family enjoyed the benefits of cutting out fat. I, for one, was trim and taut and happy to be me. The last thing on my mind was dieting. It just seemed not to be an issue any more. I figured we had this healthy living thing sewn up.

I began modelling at the age of twenty. Even though I always had a steady stream of work (mainly runway), I still lacked confidence. I had a serious self-image problem from all the years of yoyo dieting.

I think it's important at this point to let you know that I never weighed two-hundred-and-something pounds. The sort of weight I am talking about gaining amounts to a couple of dress sizes up and down. That is not to say that if you are more than a few sizes larger than your desired weight that this lifestyle won't work for you – *it will*.

> The majority of overweight Australians aren't obese – they are just a few sizes bigger than they'd like to be.

The *Fat Free Forever!* lifestyle has been designed in such a way that it is as effective in dropping the odd kilo as it is in dropping 50 kilos or even more.

After beginning work with one of Sydney's leading personal training companies, I learnt some interesting facts about body shaping. Because I wasn't all that excited by what I saw in the mirror, I set a new goal and I knew I couldn't (and didn't want to) starve myself to do it!

> I threw away my bathroom scales, and took out my tape measure and my favourite pair of jeans!

I did this because muscle tissue weighs up to three times more than fat. Because I knew I was losing fat and gaining muscle tissue, the scales would appear inaccurate, and could make even the most motivated person feel like giving up completely. My trusty tape measure and favourite pair of jeans saved the day. Each Sunday morning before church, I would try on my favourite jeans until they fit like a comfy glove. They went from 'breathe-in-and-squeeze-and-forget-it', to 'they're-on-but-don't-ask-me-to-sit-down', to 'Wow!-what-a-babe!' *(so I was told!)*. Reaching this goal was so incredibly rewarding!

I set my goal – and I achieved it without swaying! I lost inches and felt wonderful. It took a complete focus of mind and a determination.

> I had to make choices to reach my goal.

I applied the fat free principles, together with a healthy eating plan where I was having five small meals a day, plus walking. I fully achieved my goal.

I don't care to count the number of years I spent nearly killing myself in aerobic classes, week in, week out. It wasn't until I slowed down and took part in some *steady exercise*, at the rate my body worked best, that I saw the *fat burning* results *I wanted*.

I continued modelling right up until I was three months pregnant with my twin boys, Bentley and Beau. Knowing that fat cells can be laid down four times through a woman's life – early childhood, adolescence, pregnancy and menopause – I knew that if I kept my fat intake to a minimum while pregnant, I wouldn't have to work so hard afterwards. I did, however, increase my healthy eating!

I started writing this book back then. I can recall so many times I had to stop writing and run to the bathroom, because I had such awful *morning-afternoon-night* sickness! I didn't think I'd *ever* finish writing recipes! The thought of food used to make me so ill.

Thinking back to the early morning starts – sometimes 4.30 am, when I would be standing in my kitchen, barefoot and very pregnant, preparing lunch for some clients – I have to laugh. It's so rewarding seeing the fantastic results that were achieved.

But even with the knowledge I'd already gained, I put on 40 kilos during the pregnancy. By the end of the pregnancy I'd reached 100 kilos and outgrown XXL maternity clothes. It took me until the boys were 18 months old before it was all gone! That's when the cover shot of this book of me in the red swimsuit was photographed, and where the whole success of the book began.

Around that time, sadly, I found myself as a single

mum of twins – something that I never dreamt would happen to me. I have much compassion for people in the same situation. One thing that I have learnt first hand is that it's okay to have a new beginning. A wonderful new beginning for me and my boys was meeting and marrying my husband Jonathan.

Jonathan is a wonderful man and we love 'doing life' together. Jonathan and his beautiful daughter Rachel (who's now my beautiful daughter!) brought real joy and a sense of completion to Ben's, Beau's and my life. Completion, that is, until I fell pregnant on our honeymoon (not planned!) with our beautiful daughter, Bella. I put on 38.5 kilos with that pregnancy, so I had to 'get rid of it' once again.

I've never found that weight just 'falls off'. I haven't found any lying around my house, and when I go for a walk down the street, I haven't seen any falling to the ground! I have always had to 'get rid of it' with *purpose and precision*. If that's true for you, I'm sure you too will really benefit from the *Fat Free Forever!* lifestyle.

I guess my life's story is really my strength. Although I always try to identify with people's pain, I'm not prepared to leave people in their pain. It's great to identify with a problem, but that's not enough to fix it. It's my heart's desire to motivate and encourage you, so you can really enjoy seeing the results – long-term.

Fat Free Forever! tells you specifically WHAT to do, WHEN to do it, and HOW it should be done. And, unlike many other books on this subject, it clearly explains the most important factor – WHY.

> There's nothing as important as grasping a *reason* for doing something to enable you to put it into practice, *for life*!

Finding the keys to this great body shaping lifestyle has been a great learning process for me, and a combination of effort and determination, but it has all paid off. After reading *Fat Free Forever!* you will also know there is *always* a point of reference to come back to – a balance – *Fat Free Forever!* Even if you're pregnant, sick, or just completely off the rails for a while with your eating, it's always here to come back to.

It's my strong desire that you take part in it personally, and make it part of your life.

My close relationship with God is the 'secret to my success'. God has given me the ability to change my way of life, and I know you can too. I know that faith is being sure of what I hoped for, even though I couldn't see the results yet. It's definitely a combination of 'faith' and 'hard work'.

Working with some of the weirdest and most wonderful bodies made me determined to find out all there is to know about what makes great bodies great. Through study and working closely with a number of body shaping experts, I became aware of a phenomenon. It was nearly as amazing as eating fat free, but has been kept a much bigger secret.

> If I cut out all starchy carbohydrates after around 3 pm, my body would strip fat much more quickly and efficiently than any other method I'd tried.

Increasing cardiovascular activity (walking, cycling, etc) also aids greatly in the fight against fat.

Fat free living, combined with limited starchy carbohydrates and focused body shaping exercise, now gave me a wider scope for helping people.

Once the *Fat Free Forever!* body shaping lifestyle was developed, it was simply a matter of applying it and always checking back to the reference point I knew would always bring me into line, without cheating, and in the shortest amount of time. Everyone needs a lifestyle that works for them. *Fat Free Forever!* is that lifestyle.

Five years ago, when *Fat Free Forever!* was first published here in Australia, people weren't as aware of the awesome benefits of cutting out starches at night. Fortunately, now people are reaping the benefits of the *Fat Free Forever!* lifestyle.

Size 10 swimsuit model feeling great (pre-pregnancy!)

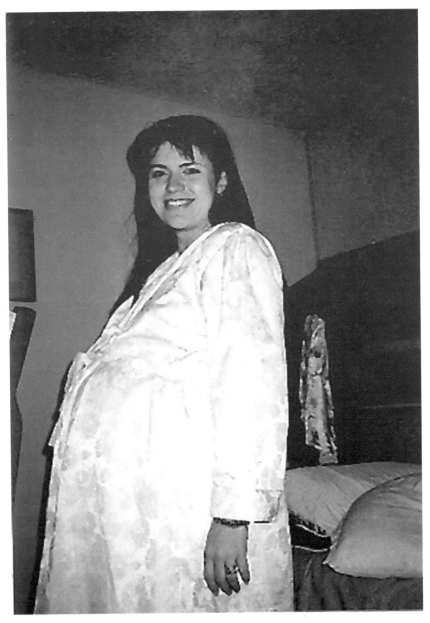

If this extraordinarily busy mother of twins can do it
YOU CAN too!

Introduction

If someone told you there is a way to never be fat again, and it comes down to a simple equation – you'd do it, wouldn't you?

limited starchy carbs   +   more
and fat free food   exercise

= A FAT FREE BODY (YOURS!)

Although I have worked as a personal trainer, it is not the only background to this book. It's more than that. It's trial and error and the experiences of myself and other people. After all, who ever really changed from just knowing something and not actually applying it to their life?

My experience is that people want to know WHAT to do, WHEN to do it, and *exactly* HOW it should be done. I wrote *Fat Free Forever!* for you. Most people are busy and often disheartened by countless failed attempts at dieting. All they really want is to be healthy, look great, and eat well – forever.

> You cannot take off your body what you keep putting in your mouth!

My theory is, if you can see the fat, it's too much. As there are enough natural fats in foods, I have designed recipes and methods around utilising this minimal amount of unseen fat in cooking. Not one recipe has any added oil, butter or cream.

I've created plenty of fat free recipes to tempt any tastebud, lighten the load off any heart, and to shape any body. What's also unique about this book is its coding system. Each recipe is coded for the best time of day to eat a particular meal. The codes are user friendly, and play a major role in the whole body shaping lifestyle.

As your metabolism works more efficiently earlier in the day, I want to encourage you to eat larger meals earlier in the day and smaller, lighter meals in the evening.

> It's not just what you eat
> (although this is obviously important),
> but also the time of day you eat it.

This is one of the absolute keys to getting your body into great shape, and is explained in detail throughout *Fat Free Forever!*

Anyone who's been on any type of diet will be happily surprised at the amount of food I am suggesting should be eaten each day. Often people under-eat, which causes the slowing down of their metabolism, which in turn causes the storage of body fat to increase. This is what the method of 'starving to be slim' can do!

The whole aim of a personal training service is to provide personal service. Obviously this can't be done through a book, so I'm willing to cross the line. The reason this book is different from other books on this subject is that *Fat Free Forever!* has been produced in the style of a training manual, which will enable you to adapt the *Fat Free Forever!* principles to your lifestyle *and* make it personal to you.

It's simple once you understand it. The WHAT, WHEN, HOW and WHY of *Fat Free Forever!* body shaping contained in this book are uncomplicated.

> I've included advice to help you shop,
> coded recipes to help you cook, menu planners
> to help you eat and a *Junk Day* once a week,
> to help keep you sane!

What have you been eating lately? Do you eat breakfast? Do you know your proteins from your carbohydrates? Do you even care? It is positively vital that you understand your body and what's going into it.

Just as an instruction manual is very handy and necessary to repair a television or video, we could have done well with a body shaping instruction manual at birth. It's simple reality that we just don't know enough about our bodies, so we therefore can't expect a lot from them. *Fat Free Forever!* can become your body shaping training manual.

> Without involvement, there's no commitment.
> Mark it down, asterisk it, circle it, underline it.
> No involvement, no commitment!
> Stephen R. Covey

You may be familiar with the Healthy Food Pyramid, or the Five Food Groups that were taught at school. What you need to do now is put them aside in your mind, in your cupboard, or even in the rubbush bin, while we explore the wonderful world of the body shaping food groups. I don't believe square pegs should have to be squeezed into round holes, so you will learn how to adapt these fat free principles into YOUR BODY and YOUR LIFE.

The *Fat Free Forever!* body shaping lifestyle is written in three easy stages for you to follow:

Stage 1   **Lifestyle Principles**
Easy to adapt lifestyle principles

Stage 2   **Food**
What you should eat and when, including great Fat Free Recipes

Stage 3   **Exercise**
Body shaping exercise to give you the body of your dreams

Remember, I believe in you. You *can* do this!

Life is full of choices.

If you eat often, *you will* help burn fat.

By increasing your lean protein intake, *you will* maintain muscle, and *you will* help burn fat.

By cutting down on starchy carbohydrates after 3 pm, *you will* help to speed your metabolism.

Do steady, focused exercise, and *you will* burn fat and shape up.

I've done the lot – and now it's *your turn!*

Welcome to the world of being *Fat Free Forever!*

Stage

1

Lifestyle Principles

Chapter 1

Freedom Forever!

Here's a thought that most people can relate to: *I do what I know I shouldn't do and I don't do what I know I should do.*

It's a very common human dilemma.

> What I don't understand about myself is that
> I decide one way, but then act another,
> doing things I absolutely despise...
> I realise that I don't have what it takes.
> I can will it, but I can't *do it*.
> I decide to do good, but I don't *really* do it;
> I decide not to do bad, but then I do it anyway.
> My decisions, such as they are, don't result in actions...
>
> Romans 7
>
> The Message

We know what we *shouldn't* do. We shouldn't:

- binge eat
- not eat
- eat and throw up or take laxatives
- eat too much junk
- eat fat
- sit around doing nothing
- tell ourselves we're fat, ugly and useless!

Many of us also know what it is that we *should* do. We should:

- eat right
- exercise
- believe we can do it!

I want you to say the following statement out loud, to yourself: 'I'm not perfect and I don't have to be either!'

In the game called LIFE, there are rules we have to play by. For every action or game play in life, there is either a positive or a negative reaction or consequence. If we don't play according to the rules, we suffer the consequences. It's our choice.

Life is full of good and bad choices, but it's also full of good and bad consequences. It's an escapable fact. If you overeat or undereat, on a regular basis, you'll not only bear the fruit of that behaviour by becoming overweight or underweight, but you will also be guilt-ridden and bound in your conscience, because you've crossed the line that you were never meant to cross. The game of life is meant to be lived and enjoyed. It's also meant to be fruitful. If your life is anything but enjoyable and fruitful, perhaps it's time to take stock and look at what is holding you back.

This book is not about *perfection*.
It's about *freedom*.

My mission in life is to see people set free in order to live their lives the way they were created to live them.

We were all born into this world full of potential. The sense of that potential is so evident in young children that it can sometimes come as a shock. I once said to my four-year-old daughter Bella, 'You're beautiful', and she said back to me, 'Yes Mummy'. I remember it surprising me for a moment. I then thought about it. There is absolutely no reason on earth why Bella wouldn't believe she is beautiful. She's four years old and all she's been told is that she is beautiful. No-one has put her down; she hasn't put herself down. Life hasn't knocked the 'stuffing' out of her.

We've all felt at times that we have been knocked over, but we don't need to be knocked out. Picture one of those silly clowns that, no matter how many times you hit it, bounces back to the upright position. If it's easy enough for a plastic clown, it should be easy enough for us. Just don't let your feet ever leave the ground!

To some people, being a couple of kilos overweight is enough to put them in a spin. Others can be 50 kilos overweight and be completely oblivious to how dangerous it is to their health. It's all relative.

I don't like being five kilos overweight, let alone being 50 kilos overweight. I had to really watch my thoughts when I put on a lot of weight, especially with my last pregnancy. I had to be careful not to take on the mindset of 'obesity', although my weight was right up there! All this would do would be to keep me trapped further and longer.

Talk about a treadmill! Some people are on a treadmill 24 hours a day, 7 days a week, 365 days a year. But it's not the walking, running or jogging variety. It's the I-need-to-do-something-about-my-body-but-can't-seem-to-get-motivated variety! That's a treadmill I want to help you get off!

Something that I have learned is that putting a name to something gives it an identity. When I was a teenager, my eating was rather disorderly, or not in order. But I didn't consider myself to have an eating disorder. There is a difference between disorderly eating and an eating disorder. The difference is in the crossing of the line. I had mild anorexia, but didn't recognise it. To me, it's what Karen Carpenter died of, and that wasn't going to happen to me!

There is a point at which a line is crossed, and that line is either into the 'over' (obesity/binge eating) category, or into the 'under' (anorexia/bulimia) category. I basically played near the 'under' line as a teenager, but I never crossed over to the point of no return. There is a big difference, and that's why people find it difficult and sometimes impossible to cross back over that line.

For example, on a scale of 1 to 10, with 1 being mild and 10 being severe, you may have an issue relating to the way you look and feel. Even a score of 1 or 2 means that you are not completely *free*. A score of 1 or 2 is enough to stop most people from fulfilling their potential in life.

After the birth of my last baby Bella, I was up very close to the 'over' line. It would have been easy to cross over and stay overweight forever. I had to make choice after choice to go down, slowly and surely. It's when people cross over the line that the term eating disorder really applies.

Society became very aware of eating disorders when Princess Diana began to talk about her struggle with bulimia, back in 1995.

Eating disorders in their various forms are serious and dangerous. At any given *Fat Free Forever!* seminar, there are always people who are *overweight* and also people who are *underweight*. I'm very aware of the fact that people struggle at both ends of the spectrum.

It's my heart's desire to see people set free in all areas of eating, be it over or under. There is a great need to address this issue before we get into the practical side of the *Fat Free Forever!* lifestyle. I call it my mission from the inside out.

Most people in my field of work expend copious amounts of energy working from the outside to the inside.

'Lose weight, feel great!'

'Lose weight, meet a mate!'

'Lose weight, eat some cake!'

'Lose weight, succeed in life!'

An eating disorder, whether mild or severe, starts somewhere. It is not a physical condition, or even merely an emotional or mental condition. An eating disorder, I believe, starts from a condition of the heart.

All little girls dream of being princesses. I dreamt of being a princess, although the dream of being a princess was definitely far, far away. I grew up in a very loving home with a very loving family. For any of you who have sisters, you may be able to relate to the normal sibling rivalry I grew up with. Unfortunately though, because my sister was (and still is) a stunning green-eyed blonde, and I was a dark-eyed brunette, the princess theme didn't quite fit my mould.

So, during childhood games I was relegated to play the part of the prince, or the slave, or even worse, the wicked witch. This was mainly due to the fact I was the youngest, but back then all I could imagine it was to do with was the colour of my hair and eyes – the way I looked.

In the seventies in Australia, the ethnic minority of immigrants weren't treated with a great deal of respect. I know because I was often mistaken for one. I was called 'wog' and other unkind names, which are now very politically incorrect!

At the same time, my parents told me I was beautiful. So, rather than becoming confused, wondering who was right and who was wrong, I believed the voice of negativity which told me I was different, which made me feel really ugly and unacceptable. I was too young to know any different.

It's laughable now, especially when I look back on many years of career success as a model. I was unusual, I guess – not a classic blonde and blue-eyed Aussie chick. When the dark exotic look came in, and the European influence became more a way of life here, I was booked for a lot of work on the best catwalks this country had to offer. Even though I was receiving a great deal of work as a model, I still struggled with my self-worth. It wasn't really tied up in my looks, or how much money I was paid. It was much deeper than that.

I needed someone to show me the way to freedom. For me everything changed at the point where I chose to believe God's word and what it had to say about me, and my life. We can hear a message and walk away and nothing changes. We need to *listen* to that message and *apply* what it says, so we can become all that we are on this planet to be. The message that changes *your* life might be this book!

The fact that I am a living testimony really helps my endeavour to help you! I have walked this walk and want to show you how beneficial and life changing it can be. My test in life has become my testimony. I love being free!

You may have had an issue with body image, over-eating, undereating, dieting or all of the above. Let's see if we can't smash the chains of entrapment and bring some *freedom* into your life. It's about time!

The first step to take is a 'reality check' on the things that could hold you back. Some of the things that you may need to deal with are:

- issues relating to obesity (being more than 20% above the ideal body-weight for your height)
- various forms of eating disorders (anorexia, bulimia, or binge eating)

Understanding what these things are and working towards removing them and their effects from your life is a top priority.

It's important to launch into the *Fat Free Forever!* body shaping lifestyle from a position of strength, ie having a healthy opinion of yourself. Even if you would like to improve certain aspects of your body shape, it's important to have a healthy body image to begin with.

Body image is basically:

- how you see or picture yourself
- how you feel that other people perceive you
- what you see in the mirror and believe
- how you feel about your physical appearance

The media has a huge part to play in the negative perceptions of our body image. We are constantly bombarded with 'perfection', and are encouraged to strive for the same. We in the western world place a high value upon appearance. If you are attractive, you must be worth more. It's just not the truth.

As parents, we need to be very careful about how we conduct ourselves in front of our children, including small children. If we are constantly dieting, or putting ourselves down, what are we saying to our children? Be careful, please.

The world of dieting is madness. Take your mind away from the concept of dieting, and engage it in a complete change of lifestyle. That's what *Fat Free Forever!* is all about.

One thing that I have found with people who have suffered from eating disorders is that although they want to be better, they are terribly afraid of getting fat. I can understand that thought process. I honestly can.

Of all the people I have met who have suffered from an eating disorder, most have said the same thing, and that is that doctors have tried to get them to gain *any* weight, and thus put them on high fat, high carbohydrate diets.

I believe there is another solution that will not compromise the health of the individual. The *Fat Free Forever!* lifestyle is designed to give people lean muscle gain and fat loss, and for them to have loads of energy. The under-eaters that I have put on the *Fat Free Forever!* lifestyle have really enjoyed it because it means that they can eat and put on weight, but not put on fat – which is what they are afraid of, and why they have the eating disorder in the first place.

I am not a doctor and I respect those who are. I just don't necessarily agree that the methods of old which are used currently are going to be of benefit to those whose struggle is not within their bodies, but within how they see themselves. They don't want to get fat, so making them eat lots of fat isn't going to help them! All it does is alienate them from getting free and make the situation worse.

Most of us crave chocolate *more* than we crave freedom! We go for the quick fix. Instant gratification. Short-term gain (the taste of chocolate) and long-term pain (a life of out-of-control eating).

Why? Because as human beings *we do what we know we shouldn't do* and *we don't do what we know we should do*. We know what is good and what is bad, but we need to get *free*. True freedom is about being comfortable in your own skin. Whatever is holding you back needs to be rectified. Speak kindly to yourself and live the *Fat Free Forever!* lifestyle, and freedom will be within your grasp.

Below are some ways you can improve your self-esteem:

- Find something you like about yourself – grow in awareness of your positive attributes.
- When you buy fashion magazines, decide not to measure yourself against the size 1 models!
- Eat healthily – live the *Fat Free Forever!* lifestyle.
- Exercise regularly – you won't know how fantastic you will feel until you get out and do it!
- Replace bad habits with good habits, *for life*!
- Be honest with yourself, and refuse to put yourself down. If you can't say something nice about yourself, don't say anything at all.
- Be grateful for how you were made. Recognise that a bulge to you may be a curve to someone else. Curves are beautiful, so don't despise them.

Smile at the future and believe that you can achieve your dreams – forever.

Chapter

2

Great
Expectations

You will want to know what you should expect if you follow the *Fat Free Forever!* body shaping lifestyle. You will lose fat, retain muscle tissue, lower cholesterol, have increased energy, and you will sleep soundly.

> You will eat better, sleep better, work better, feel better and look better – and everyone will notice!

Firstly, if you follow what I've outlined, even if you cannot manage to take part in any exercise, you will lose body fat. Basically, what doesn't go in your mouth – *fat* – has to come off your body. And what's left underneath the fat is your body's muscle tissue, which gives you your shape – so you don't want to lose it!

Because muscle outweighs fat by three times, it's

important not to weigh yourself constantly, like you may have done in the past with other diets. Instead, grab your favourite piece of clothing that you wish you could fit into, and try it on no more than once a week.

Also, if you can, go to the gym and have a FAT TEST done. You will be surprised at the amount of fat lost after being on the *Fat Free Forever!* lifestyle for a few weeks. You may not see dramatic results in weight or size loss before then, because you won't be losing water or muscle tissue, which is the bulk of the weight lost on regular diets.

The reality is that stubborn fat is always the last to leave your body.

> You will be laying down *fat free* foundation stones by sticking to the *Fat Free Forever!* lifestyle. It's a worthwhile lifestyle investment.

This means that if you lose your way later on, you can always find help again with this lifestyle, and it should only take you about one third of the time to regain your great body shape.

Don't expect the same results you've had with other diets. You may even feel like giving up after a week, but once you've pushed through, around the 21-day mark, you will be firing! It will become a part of you and your lifestyle.

The body's metabolism is truly remarkable. I liken it to knowing when you need to go to the bathroom. Once your body is in tune with proper eating, it lets you know – loud and clear – when it wants to eat. For the first week or so, you will probably have to keep checking what to eat and when to eat it. After that, your body will *tell you* what it needs and when.

This lifestyle is part of an education process. I'm educating your mind; it's up to you to educate your body. This is the only way you'll change your body's metabolism into super-turbo mode!

At around the three-week mark, you will start to see a difference, and you will certainly feel different:

'*I am sleeping so soundly now.*'

'*I have a tremendous amount of energy throughout the day.*'

These comments are from normal, everyday people – not even necessarily those who are able to go to the gym each day to exercise. It's simply due to proper eating.

If you cannot exercise (I know what it's like to have small kids, and how restrictive that can be), this lifestyle *will* work for you. However, by adding some focused exercise, such as walking for 45 to 60 minutes a day, three to five times a week, you will lose even more body fat.

And, if you are really keen, try to get to a gym where there are good weights machines to start sculpting your body.

Everyone wants to know what makes great bodies great. To simplify the issue, it's basically fat free eating, limiting the amount of starchy carbohydrates (especially at night), taking part in steady exercise, such as walking, and hitting the gym to do weights about three times a week. This is an optimum plan for an optimum body.

At about the six to eight week mark, even without exercise, you will notice a real difference in your body's shape. This will motivate and catapult you into the next phase. I try to only set goals that are around the six to eight week mark – something achievable. If you know the truth of what to expect at the outset, then this training manual will not only assist your motivation, but you will not stop, because it's happening on schedule for you, and you will see great results.

> Because I've been on the receiving end of living the *Fat Free Forever!* lifestyle, the results are always enough to motivate me to keep going.

Imagine setting a body shaping goal and actually achieving it! It does wonders for your self-esteem, not to mention your body shape.

> Begin with the end in mind.
> Stephen R. Covey

Be realistic in your goal setting, and remember the old saying, 'Slow and steady wins the race'. It will work for you. Don't be in a big hurry to lose weight too quickly, or else (as usual) it won't stay off.

Sit back and dream about the type of body shape you want and the size you want to be, and then start planning for it.

Chapter 3

Establish Your Enemies

It's the war against the bulge, so it's important to establish your enemies and be ready for combat. What are your enemies?

> 1. Fat
> 2. Starchy carbohydrates after 3 pm
> 3. Under-exercising or over-exercising

Fat is one of the greatest body shaping enemies – in fact it's definitely the worst, and it's important to recognise this first of all. Search it out, track it down and eliminate it.

The second lethal body shaping enemy is consuming *starchy carbohydrates* – bread, pasta, rice and potatoes and, for the midnight munchers, cereal – at the wrong time of day, which is basically any time after 3 pm.

Under-exercising or no exercise at all will lead to a very sluggish metabolism. *Over-exercising* will lead to burn-out and potential injuries. The balance will lead to a great metabolism and a lifestyle of sensible and effective exercise.

These three enemies really are a combination that can cause damage. Discontinuing one without the others simply will not help you achieve the body shape of your dreams.

The myth surrounding starchy carbohydrates – 'energy foods' – is that you need huge amounts of them to function each day. The only problem with this is that unless you are training like an ironman or elite athlete, you shouldn't be eating breakfast cereal like one! Unless you are extremely active – and 90% of us are not – then energy foods, including bananas, will be stored in your body. This unused glut of energy foods is stored in the form of fat.

Nine times out of ten, if you are feeling lethargic and needing what you think is an energy boost, your body is dehydrated and simply needs a water refuelling, and could probably do with a brisk walk around the block!

Firstly you need to assess your body type (see Body Types and Metabolism, p. 42), and only take in food that you need to function healthily, to give you enough fibre and energy to fight the fight against fat, and nothing more.

You may well be watching your fat intake and reducing your evening meal, but it's important that you realise that the 'fat free' and the 'no starchy carbs after 3 pm' theories are what's going to make the difference to everything you've ever tried before.

The third body shaping enemy, and this may come as a surprise, is the wrong kind of *exercise*. Make sure that when you exercise, you take it steady and don't get breathless. Now this doesn't mean that you shouldn't work up a sweat, but it does mean that you should be working at a pace you can stick at, and not have to give up in case you keel over.

The minute you become too breathless, you will be burning carbohydrates and *not fat*. So slow down to around 110 to 130 beats a minute, and go for longer if you can. I'll be covering why this is so important in Stage 3: Exercise (starting on p. 122). Don't miss it!

The fight against body fat is a real combination of efforts. For some examples of elimination, and of what works and what doesn't, please read on.

Example 1: one-out-of-three

You attend high-impact aerobics classes a few times a week and come home to a nice bowl of pasta or rice, with absolutely no fat. It's okay, but you're still not losing any weight.

Example 2: two-out-of-three

You attend high-impact aerobics classes a few times a week and come home to a medium-sized serving of protein and a small serving of fibrous carbohydrates (broccoli, carrots, snow peas, corn, etc), with absolutely no fat. It's okay, but you're still losing only a little weight.

Example 3: three-out-of-three

You walk for 45–60 minutes a day, three to five times a week, and at night you eat a medium-sized serving of protein and a small serving of fibrous carbohydrates, with absolutely no fat. You are finally losing weight – and it's not water or muscle, it's *fat*!

> It's when things seem worst that you
> MUST NOT quit!
> Jake Steinfeld

We've all heard it and we all know it. Now, *what are we going to do about it?* You need to address the real issues.

LACK OF TIME

Probably one of the biggest and most common problems faced by most people is time – or lack thereof. It could be a genuine excuse or it may just be one that rolls off the tongue as easy as, 'And an extra large fries with my double cheese and bacon burger, please!'

I want you to examine closely the excuses you have used to avoid getting in shape, whether they are valid or hilarious, and make a decision to make some changes.

LACK OF MONEY

If it's lack of money, then this book has certainly fixed that problem. Instead of having to pay anything from $50 to $150 or more per hour for your very own personal trainer – this book is an inexpensive yet worthwhile and highly valuable investment.

LACK OF MOTIVATION

If it's general lack of motivation, I want to ask you to do something. Think about how long you have been battling with your general body shape, be it weeks, months or years. Then, think about the amount of time you would have to exercise to make a great difference to your body's shape. Now, I want you to compare the two thoughts! One definitely outweighs the other.

PROCRASTINATION

If you have been battling for, say, five years, and you now know that in less than a year, you could look and feel awesome, it would be a worthwhile investment of time, money and motivation.

A friend who has battled with 'bigness' all her life shared proudly with me that she is so glad she started – and *finished*.

Her starting became her initial motivation, and the results from her efforts became her continuing motivation, until now, when she has far exceeded her original goals, because she decided to blow the sides off her preconceived thoughts of herself as a big person.

TIREDNESS

There's more to it than meets the eye when it comes to taking good care of your body. It's much more than exercise, it's also good eating habits and plenty of rest as well. For some of us, it's also important to take time to relax and unwind, to alleviate the stresses of the day (I can certainly relate to this one!).

Sometimes I look in the mirror at my face and think 'yuck!', because all I can see when I look is that I haven't been taking care of myself. Lack of sleep, too many cups of tea and not enough exercise. That's when I take a grip and say, I'm going to do something about this – *starting TODAY!*

Each of us require different amounts of attention to function properly each day. Post-kids, I can get by with five to six hours sleep, although mostly my body craves eight or more hours. And some days, I have to have an afternoon rest, because I can't think straight because of tiredness. This is not good!

YOUR PAST

One of the most common issues I face when dealing with people who are overweight is that there appear to be all manner of reasons for their physical condition. Be it an unhappy childhood, unhappy marriage, a traumatic event, or just pure 'genetics', there's always been something to take hold of and 'blame'.

Somewhere along the line, taking care of yourself has become the furthest priority from your mind, as the other issues and problems have crowded in around you. These issues and problems need to be released before you can move on.

Go through the process of *establishing your enemies*, and deal with these things *once and for all*. While you are not dealing with your internal pain, you are also not dealing with your external anguish. While you continue in your grief, your body will continue to grow further and further out of shape.

> Nothing is too tough for people who really want to change!

Go ahead, turn your stress into strategy and then you will experience victory in your life.

NEGATIVE WORDS

Your enemies may actually be words that have been spoken over your life which have formed a frame in which you have been living. For instance, my friend who won her battle had always been big, and had always been thought of and talked about as being big. It was going to be difficult not only to change her physical shape, with all the time and energy that goes into that, but also to bring about change in the opinions of others around her.

She had to be prepared to take up the challenge and win.

WORTHLESSNESS

Another great enemy is self-doubt and feelings of worthlessness. If you have no confidence in your ability to complete anything and don't feel worthy anyway, you don't stand much of a chance, now, do you?

You need to see yourself as you were created to be.

If that means that we have to get below a few layers of 'winter coat', then let's begin that process slowly but surely.

You are not alone. I understand what it is like to have tried and failed every diet and exercise program under the sun, and have met many other people who have failed as well.

Whatever your body shaping enemy is or has been, be assured that it can be conquered.

YOUR ENEMIES OPERATE BY STEALTH

Are you aware of how much damage the Stealth Bomber plane can do in a war? Plenty! That's because you can't see it coming!

The invisible enemy is probably the most dangerous. Go looking for those things which, until you read this chapter, remained incognito. Search those things out and target them. Together we're going to overcome these body shaping enemies – once and for all!

Chapter

Body Types and Metabolism

There are three body types, and most people's lifestyles have led them to look like a mixture of two of them.

Ectomorph	naturally thin eats anything has difficulty keeping any weight on often nervy and hyperactive *Example*: Twiggy or Kate Moss
Mesomorph	naturally lean but holds a great shape athletic build has little problem with food *Example*: Cindy Crawford or Elle McPherson

Endomorph   naturally round
puts on weight by looking at food
has a hard time dieting
Example: Marilyn Monroe or Raquel
Welch

Ectomorph, endomorph or mesomorph. Which one (*or combination of two*) are you? Well, whichever one you are, *it doesn't matter!* There is a great body toning routine just for you! Initially, your body type and metabolism will determine where you start with everything. If you are an ectomorph or endomorph, you may not have as much natural get-up-and-go as a classic mesomorph, but you are able to work towards anything.

Then again, a mesomorph who is not at all athletically inclined, who would much prefer to watch the basketball than play it, is going to be far less fit than an ectomorph who has been running marathons for the past five years. It's all relative when it comes to exercise.

> Even if you are born with it, if you don't use it, you will lose it!

It's difficult for someone who was born an endomorph, and who has trained their way to being more of a mesomorph, to watch a classic mesomorph eating huge amounts of burgers and fries, never exercising, and looking exceptionally good, even at the age of 50!

The advantage that both the endomorph and ectomorph have over the mesomorph is the inbred ability and drive to do something to improve their body shape and fitness levels. It's called tenacity and it's a positive attribute.

This can work positively on their behalf to assist them to focus in other areas of life. Some mesomorphs don't grow up worrying about their physical condition, until one day all that bad eating and lack of exercise catches up with them.

For anyone who has been overweight for any significant period of time, life has been tough for you. The consuming and constraining anguish of each day rolls on, with the pressure that you have to do something about your weight. If this is you, you could start by stopping your thoughts about your size, and concentrating rather on your health.

Please don't instantly presume that you are naturally an *endomorph* just because you are trying to lose weight. Poor eating habits can push you into the 'hard-to-lose' category, but you may well be genetically one of the other types or, more likely, a mixture.

The truth is that each body type is beautiful. When people who are naturally curvy starve themselves to be like a stick-figure, they have gone too far. Everyone needs a revelation of who they are and what they are meant to look like (taking into consideration height, bone structure, etc), so they can set body shaping goals accordingly.

One is not better than another; each body shape is unique and beautiful.

> Only your metabolism and muscles burn fat.

Your metabolism is like an engine that constantly runs, keeping your body working, burning fuel for body functions and energy. It fluctuates throughout the day, depending on certain factors, including the time of day you eat and exercise.

In the fight against fat, it's vital to keep your metabolism up as much as possible. When it slows naturally, as it does at night so you can sleep, it's important that you eat only low-energy foods so they are not stored as fat.

You should eat larger meals in the earlier part of the day and smaller meals later in the day. This works *with* your body, rather than against it. It's a much easier method of losing weight and maintaining a long-term healthy lifestyle.

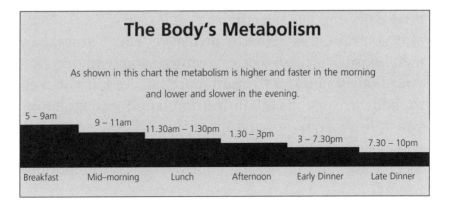

If your metabolism is slow from either genetics or poor eating habits, don't presume that it will never speed up. Some of the best success stories have come from people who have been overweight all of their lives, for both of the above reasons. The great news is, in a very short time, no matter how long you have been overweight, you should be able to lose not only the weight you want to, but also expect that your metabolism will become faster and more efficient.

Without addressing the real problem of body fat, by trying diets here and there, you are virtually putting a bandage over a compounding problem. The only way to cure this problem is to naturally change your body's metabolism once and for all. It may mean you must have more diligence in the beginning, but you can increase your body's metabolism over time, which in the long term will make life much more enjoyable for you.

Your body has a base metabolism that is generally around 1000 calories a day, give or take a few hundred. This is the minimum amount your body burns to keep you alive. Any activity beyond this point will add to your total daily energy expenditure.

If you raise this figure by increasing your natural base metabolism through correct eating, you will see how your body will instantly burn more fat. And, if you were to add sensible metabolism-stimulating eating habits, you will see even more fat disappear. Of course, exercise will speed things up even more by stimulating your metabolism and increasing your overall consumption of energy.

This book is written for everybody, which means it's for you. Whether you are a mesomorph who needs to become healthier on the inside and outside, or an ectomorph who needs to train for energy, or a mixture between the two!

All body types alike are always on the look-out for something that will work. Even an ectomorph can suffer from '*potbellyitis*'. By the way, don't ever feel restricted by a definition, and remember *your* personal best! These definitions (endomorph, mesomorph and ectomorph) are just for your interest, and not to make you feel bad about yourself.

I remember one of my clients was so thrilled to hear about this book, because he couldn't do any form of exercise as a result of injuries he'd sustained during training over a period of years.

When I got to the cause of the problem, I found that he had been running for fat loss and fitness, but he'd been running with injured shins, and continued to do so, until he basically couldn't walk. This is a great example of someone who not only didn't know their body, but didn't listen to it either.

In this case, short-term pain was not long-term gain. In fact, it was quite the opposite. At times we exercise madly in the hope that getting it over and done with quickly will make a difference in our lives. The reality is that this is very rarely the case.

Once you know your body, you will come to realise that not everyone is born into exercise, and nor do they need to be. We don't need a long history of sports involvement, and we don't even have to like it when we start. We do have to find a way of beginning and of nurturing our exercise habits, then the rest will take care of itself!

You need to listen to your body. As you exercise, your body is constantly responding, telling you how you are progressing, and how well you are doing. Pay attention when you body tells you to slow down or stop.

Remember, an exercise program should be intended to make you feel healthy and well. It should not be used as an endurance contest, unless, of course, you want to be an elite athlete.

Following are *3 keys to body shaping success*. Keeping to these keys will make your choices much easier.

3 KEYS TO
BODY SHAPING SUCCESS

1 Instead of weighing everything on your plate, weigh it in your mind.
(Am I satisfied? Do I need to eat this?)

2 Consider the effort required for your body to burn what you're about to eat.
(1 hour walk = 400 calories or a medium-sized plate of healthy food.)

3 Will you have time or be motivated enough to burn what you're about to eat *after* you've eaten it?
(Exercise can be a great appetite suppressant!)

Chapter 5

Motivate Me!

The average dieter stays on a diet for approximately three weeks – maximum. What happens after that? Usually, because they have deprived themselves so much, they end up eating far in excess of what they were eating before, just to balance what they have missed out on. Can you relate to this so far? We of good intentions!

That's normal for dieters on a calorie restrictive diet, but abnormal for you with your new *Fat Free Forever!* lifestyle.

GOAL SETTING

The key to getting this lifestyle to work for you is to establish goals and reach benchmarks. Your long-term goal, the end result, realistically may take some time, but to achieve your first short-term goal will only take approximately six to eight weeks. Later in this chapter, I've listed some easy steps to help you establish your long-term goal and to achieve your short and mid-term goals.

You need to set goals according to who you are. For instance, if you are naturally very curvy, don't set a goal to look like Twiggy (a classic ectomorph). That's impractical and will be demotivating for you!

Your long-term body shaping goal will determine how many short and mid-term goals you need to set yourself. Only set them one at a time, however, and remember when setting them that *you are only human.*

> Competing with others is sport.
> Competing with yourself is the true test.

The key for me has been to keep the goals short and sweet. I need to have a reason to walk for an hour a day. I make it a priority because it affects the rest of my life.

I need to know that once I have reached my short or mid-term goal, I am going out to dinner somewhere really special, or I'm buying some new clothes. It's only human to need to know you will receive a reward at the end of it all. Rewards are a great motivator!

The key to all this is that the reward should come from you. You arrange it and you deliver it, and know that you've done it for yourself and not because someone who'll never understand how hard it's been for you up until now tells you to do it. Achieving your new improved body shape possibly seems like a dream at this stage. Live the lifestyle and it will become reality for you.

To retain your new, improved body shape you will still

need to be quite careful with your eating. The wonderful news is that your metabolism will be faster and you will be able to include a few more luxury indulgences every now and again.

If you feel yourself slipping, though, you know how you reached your goal, and you simply need to reapply those same simple principles.

GET A LIFE!

> The *Fat Free Forever!* lifestyle is about losing bad habits and gaining a *life!*

Fat Free Forever! has been designed in every way to make getting into shape as efficient and easy as possible. You are being offered the 100% most efficient methods to reach your goals. Out of that 100%, it's really up to you just how much you decide to do. At least you will have a mark to measure yourself against – a check point – as far as effort you've put in, versus the results you've actually achieved.

If you put in 50% effort, you will gain 50% improvement, which may be all you want. You set the pace, and you choose. If your results aren't quite up to what you'd hoped for, then it's just a matter of taking on a few per cent more effort. This is also a very good way to train an unwilling mind or body into doing what you want it to do.

This lifestyle is perfect for the busy person who wants to do as little as possible for maximum results. On its own, the nutritional section, ie the *Fat Free Forever!*

daily eating plan, has wonderful results, enabling you to achieve a great deal more than you may have thought you could, and that's without breaking into a sweat.

It would be negligent of me not to ensure that you are aware of the *100% lifestyle*, for optimum results in the shortest amount of time (*without cheating*). This of course includes some body shaping exercise – see Stage 3: Exercise, starting on p. 122.

Try and keep in the forefront of your mind why you started on this body shaping mission, and that too will help you keep on track. This may all seem overwhelming right now, but how long have you been unhappy with how you look and feel? It's time to bite the bullet and take action. The longer you think about it and wait for a miracle to drop out of the sky, the longer you are going to be unhappy. It's time to get practical and motivated to change.

It's truly amazing to see what I have seen in my business. People from all walks of life really have the same desires and needs as everyone else. Whether speaking for a large corporation, or a small group of housewives and mothers, wanting to look and feel better is universal.

You will be amazed at how many people will look to you for support. This will also motivate and encourage you to maintain your new body shape. If you want to help others in the future, your pain can now help to become someone else's gain.

> When setting your goals, please be realistic.

It's the same principle as when you travel on vacation. You always tend to pack that nice pant suit that you bought in a sale, in a rush, or that nice shimmery evening gown, two sizes too small, that you put away to wear to a romantic dinner at the exclusive resort you always dreamt about visiting.

Did you end up actually wearing these things? No! I know, because I've done this and so have you! We all think that vacation time is the golden opportunity to change habits, and get on top of all that we let snow us under every other month of the year.

The problem is that our goals for our vacation aren't realised and we end up coming home, not having worn all that stuff we packed, and not having read one single book we brought with us, and in a sense feeling like we failed.

It's the same with getting into shape. Why on earth say to yourself at 9 pm on Sunday night, after eating a large pepperoni pizza by youself, 'I'm never eating pizza ever again.' Get real! Of course you will, so it's a ridiculous statement to make. The same can be said of you desperately wanting to get in shape: 'I'm going to start in the morning with my diet, and I'm joining the gym tomorrow afternoon and I'm going to do two aerobics classes and train in the gym all before I come home tomorrow night *and* I'm going to do this *eight* days a week!'

It's more realistic if you haven't taken part in any exercise before, or for a long time, to start out slowly with a simple walking routine, maybe 30 minutes a day, two to three times each week, and then increase it. Remember though: results are directly reflected by the amount of effort you put in!

> The definition of victory:
> saying you'll do something, and actually doing it.

PERFECTION NOT REQUIRED

My main qualification for writing this book is that I do not have a perfect body! And I never will! 'Hooray,' I can hear you cheer! I am here to share some inspirational thoughts with you that will hopefully lead you to the revelation that there is no such thing as the perfect physique. Less than 2% of all bodies in the world resemble the supermodels we see adorning the pages of women's glamour magazines. This is not a real picture of what the women in the world look like.

There is a Greek word, *'Teleios'*, which interpreted means, *'perfect for now'*. That is, perfect at our own particular stage of development. We all have a personal best, and that is what we are to strive towards.

It doesn't mean that we are to strive towards a Cindy best or an Elle best or a Claudia best – it means that we are to strive for *our own personal best.*

Has this thought released you? It certainly released me!

I believe that this is a great truth and a wonderful place from which to build a great new lifestyle. You can now look at yourself, and your own personal potential, and work within your own fence, and not the one across the 'supermodel' road.

Once you understand your personal best for now, you can watch it change and grow. 'Perfect for now' means that once you have read this book, and start to live your new lifestyle, you will become fitter and more toned, and your perfection or *Teleios* will also grow with you. It is an exciting process and really is without limitations!

> I'm not one of those people who can claim they love exercise. But I do love all it does for me!
> Oprah Winfrey

I have found that at the core of most overweight people is a motivational thought that doesn't entirely revolve around themselves. Something I have found in common with many people I come into contact with is an eager desire to help others around them who are going through something that they can relate to.

For example, one of my clients who has battled with being overweight all of her life is a really lovely person, and continually talks to me about how she wants to change so that she can help and influence others to look after themselves.

I really encourage this type of outlook on life. It can only be a good thing. And it can often be the motivational point at which some people get themselves moving! To be able to do this, however, one must first become an example which others can actually follow.

Although I don't want to discourage anyone from helping others, it's important to be in a position of strength before you start trying to help others.

Victory is only sweet if you get to taste it! How do we have victory? By setting goals that are *achievable*, and then reaching them. Writing this book amidst a very busy life has meant that I have had to set goals to achieve my deadlines. The only problem with this though – and might I add that I am quite a disciplined person – was that I was setting goals that I had no way of achieving: walk for an hour, train at the gym for an hour, cook a 'fat free gourmet meal' for my family, visit my grandmother, do five loads of washing, take the kids to and from school, clean my house, iron my tea towels, counsel five people, and then spend eight hours writing books – each day! I had to do a serious reality check on my life. Once I set goals for what was humanly possible (and I am known to push that limit from time to time!), then I began to experience victory in that particular area of my life. It's the same with you. STOP setting unrealistic goals, and start experiencing victory!

A while back, it hit me suddenly that there is more to getting in shape than not being able to wear a mini-skirt for some women. If only it was a fashion problem – we could usher in the nice A-line skirt or bustle and train at will – but unfortunately the issue is far wider than this. I'm talking about thighs – you know, those pillars of strength that keep you standing, day in, day out.

A few years ago I was walking with a friend, someone who I never thought of as being overweight, although always looked solid. One day while we were walking she turned to me and said, 'What's it like to walk without your legs rubbing together?' To be quite honest, until she posed this question, I'd never really thought about it!

Since that time, I have come across many women, who aren't necessarily all that overweight, who have struggled with the same issue. It means putting on baby powder in the morning or wearing cycle shorts under a skirt, just to stop chafing, especially in summer!

Also, after having kids, nothing is quite the same, and nor should it have to be! Your tummy has just performed the miracle of its lifetime. I think it's amazing that it returns to any flattened shape at all. There are ways, though, of reducing the squidge-effect, through correct eating and some great tummy toning exercises. It's much harder if you're a Mum who's had a taut little tummy, to find that only a few years later, you seem to have a little pot belly happening.

Living the *Fat Free Forever!* lifestyle, you will find great results with your little pot belly, because most of the time, if this is the only real problem area, it can be corrected just by changing what you eat.

Now as for the back of those arms, what can I say? I know what I'm like. The slightest bit of weight on, and I cover up for no-one to see! I guess it's because I've always had kind of 'slinky' arms, and am aware of them more if they are not their 'slinky' best. 'Oh, what it would be like to wear a sleeveless top and shorts?' It would be great – and you can do it, if you want to. Just picture what you don't like, and imagine your personal best in that area. That's your long-term goal.

I guess the most amazing thing for me was returning to a bikini, only 18 months after giving birth to my twin boys, at which time I weighed in at 100 kilograms! And, no, I haven't been super-skinny all my life!

THE TIME FACTOR

Time is something that if you feel you don't have, especially when it comes to looking after your physical well-being, *you need to create*. Recently I discovered that if I was going to be able to get an hour's walk in every day, the only way I could do this so it didn't cut into the rest of my day was to get up at 5.45 am and walk from 6 am until 7 am, from Monday to Friday. This really is a very small sacrifice of an hour's sleep, compared to the wonderful benefits of getting fresh air, a fit heart, and great legs!

Nothing in life is free, including our time. In fact, if someone tells me that they want something from me and it won't cost me any money, *just a little of my time*, every warning bell in me goes into mega-alarm. I truly do understand the issue of precious time. I also understand that precious time is useless time if we can't enjoy spending it! There is absolutely no use in working, working, working, if at some stage in your life, you don't stop and start enjoying all you've been working for.

If you are working too hard to stop and look after yourself, you need to sit down and prioritise your entire life. What use is it if you lose your life because of ill-health due to a pitiful diet and lack of exercise? It's time to sit back and think about what's *really* important. *Life!*

MONEY

You know, the whole money issue when it comes to exercise is something that need not be a problem. You don't have to join a gym, although if you can afford it, they are a great way of staying motivated, and all the equipment under the sun is there at your beck and call.

If you have a roof over your head, some furniture in your house and can afford to buy a simple pair of dumb-bells, you can have the body, health and longevity of your dreams.

Don't forget, walking is free! It doesn't have to be on a $10,000 treadmill, it can be around the block, or in your local park. Stepping is also free. It doesn't have to be on a lunar-space model step machine, it can be instead of taking the elevator! Use that creative mind, which can take you shopping for a new wardrobe for next to nothing, to take you training for your new toned physique!

FAMILY COMMITMENTS

Your family are so important, and time should be spent with them. It's really difficult to exercise when you have small children, but this is only for such a short time. Soon you will be on your way. I remember just *before* my twin boys were born, I decided that after their birth, I was going to work out at the gym three days a week, take them for a walk for an hour five days a week, and train clients when they were asleep during the day.

HUH! Talk about unrealistic goals! When my twin boys were born, I was in sheer survival mode. Forget exercise, I could hardly get out of bed to walk to the bathroom, I was so exhausted. I was feeding them every couple of hours and I was up and down with them day and night. Oh, the plans of mice and men!

It took a good six month period for me to even think about any kind of exercise. I had been so preoccupied with trying to get enough sleep that it's all I could think of for the first few months. When I did start, however, I was ready for it. My babies were a little older, and I started out slowly, and included them whenever I could when I walked.

You can do plenty for your body by eating correctly, even if you can't exercise. But there is something that is irreplaceable – the invigorating feeling of exercise. Fresh air, deep breaths, worked muscles. Even if it takes some working up to, it's a worthwhile plan to include a realistic exercise routine in your life.

ESTABLISH YOUR LONG-TERM GOAL

1   You must have a dream, so start to dream if you don't have one already. *Begin with the end in mind.* Imagine the body you want to achieve. Put doubts that aren't part of the plan out of your mind, and keep a focus on what your plan is.

2   Find a photograph or clipping from a magazine which is close to the body shape you want, and put it on your fridge.

3   Tell one person what you are doing and become accountable to them.

4   Realise that what has taken you months or years to accumulate will take time and determination to lose and keep off.

5   Make a conscious choice that you aren't going to let your tastebuds rule your life any more!

STARTING YOUR FIRST WEEK

1   Grab your favourite pair of jeans or a skirt (or similar) that's one size too small, and choose one morning each week to try them on.

2   Measure yourself with a tape measure (or have someone else do it for you). Always measure at the biggest point: shoulders, chest, waist, upper hips (including lower stomach), lower hips (including bottom and upper thighs), upper arm, upper thigh, calf.

3   Remember, Junk Day is always just around the corner! Keep this at the forefront of your mind should you contemplate breaking the lifestyle.

4   Exercise as much as you can – ideally an hour's walk a day is great, along with any time you can put in at the gym or at home doing weights.

5   Only have the types of food in your house that you are allowed to eat, and none other. Keep a special stash for the kids or visitors, if you must, but don't be tempted to indulge yourself. Enjoy your Junk Day out and don't bring home any leftovers!

REACHING YOUR SHORT AND MID-TERM GOALS

1   The results you achieve will be your best motivation. Stick with it and watch! You will be eating and sleeping better, you will have more energy, and people will notice how much better you're looking. You will have a glow about you that you just don't get with dieting.

2   Measure yourself with a tape measure even less often now. Try to do it just once a month. And, if you wish, jump on the scales – but remember muscle weighs three times more than fat! Don't be discouraged!

3   Grab the next article of clothing you want to fit into and keep it handy to try on once a fortnight.

4   Your clear skin and feeling of renewed energy will be something which will help you continue, and will also enable you to do more exercise.

5   Your new lifestyle of eating without added fats will be something you will be used to by now. As soon as high doses of fats and sugars hit your system on your Junk Day, you'll really feel it!

Stage 2

Food

Chapter

6

Body Shaping Food Groups

This chapter has been designed to help you understand the different types of foods I'll be suggesting you eat, and why. Rather than listing the suggested foods in a food pyramid, *Fat Free Forever!* is more original (and practical), and goes into much more detail for you. I've explained not only what to eat, but why and how it will affect your body shape.

If you don't particularly like the food I've suggested, or if you are allergic to it, it can, in most cases, be substituted. Once you read through all the detail, you should be able to create your own personal body shaping food pyramid.

> Remember, food can be a means to an end,
> or it can be enjoyed along the way.
> Enjoy!

PROTEIN

Protein is a vital part of your daily eating plan. It also happens to be one of the most misunderstood areas of nutrition. The meat lobby expounds the virtues of the 'near-medicinal' qualities of various meats. Then there's the vegetarians, who propose life after hamburgers with lentils and soya beans. Finally there's the health fanatics, drinking shape-up shakes and miracle slimming drinks. So what is what, and who's right and who's wrong? These groups all have fairly sound reasons for their choice of protein intake. *Fat Free Forever!* goes a step further, however, to find out what is best for us in our quest for a *better body shape*.

Most people don't ask what they are eating for. By reading *Fat Free Forever!*, I presume your reason is to change your body shape, so let's look at the options for eating, in that particular context. Protein is your body's building blocks. If you took all the water out of your body, you would be left with just over 50% pure protein. Now that should give you something to think about. Your body also annually renews more than 95% of all its molecules, and every molecule is made up predominantly of protein and water. *That's how important protein is!*

Now, as impressive as that information may be, you still need to know how that relates to a better body shape. Unfortunately, most dieters forget this next very important point: muscle will only tone and shape if there is enough protein to feed it. The reason we want muscle to tone is so we will look and feel better, but even more important than that is the fact that *toned muscle is incredibly efficient at burning fat.* Muscles use fat as their fuel, so the more toned and stronger the muscles, the more efficient they are at burning fat. For example, a 4-cylinder car doesn't burn very much fuel because the cylinders are small and it is not a very powerful vehicle, but an 8-cylinder car needs many more litres of fuel because it is much more powerful. Therefore, it's obvious that by making our bodies more efficient through eating and exercising correctly, we will become more like the 8-cylinder car. We are going to turn everyday movements and activities into fat- and calorie-consuming workouts!

This is why protein consumption is so important.

In deciding which protein is best for you to eat, refer to the protein chart on p. 71, which will give you a complete guide to the best and worst proteins.

Meat Proteins

To help you better understand this section I am referring to meat proteins as any animal product, including poultry, fish and dairy products. Meat can be an excellent source of what are called 'complete proteins'. Protein is made up of amino acids, and 'complete proteins' contain all the eight essential amino acids in the quantities needed to be fully used by the body. If a food doesn't contain all the amino acids in the correct ratios, it is called an 'incomplete protein', because the body cannot use it.

You don't need to know in detail which amino acids do what. It is fairly easy to remember that all meats and dairy products have the eight essential amino acids in good amounts, and that all vegetables, fruit and grains either don't have any at all, or they are substantially lacking in them.

So from this perspective, meat proteins are a good choice. Of course, as you will read on the protein chart, some meats are a whole lot better than others because of their fat content. Generally, fish and white meat rate highest, and so should be considered before all others when choosing a protein from this category.

Vegetable Protein

As already mentioned, vegetables are not great sources of protein on their own. When it comes to consuming enough to meet your daily requirements, this can cause a problem – especially if you are exercising or are fairly active. To ensure you are getting the complete eight essential amino acids from vegetables, dried beans, peas, lentils and grains, you must eat two or more of these foods together, for example, dried beans and a grain such as brown rice or couscous.

Being a vegetarian can turn into a science of its own, learning what goes with what. At the end of the day, vegetarians will often still have consumed under the optimum daily requirements, because of the low amount of essential amino acids – gram for gram – in vegetables.

Most people know that nuts and soya beans are relatively good forms of protein. However, they are both proteins that are not readily absorbed by the body, and nuts contain large amounts of fat! AVOID THEM.

Slimming Shakes

This is an interesting area where, unfortunately, a good idea has grown into a monster! Have you ever read the contents on the labels of these drinks? You would become slimmer drinking a melted chocolate sundae.

It is, however, very easy to distinguish the good from the bad, and it is well worth the effort to do so. Protein shakes are actually your BEST option for optimum results. Providing you have selected the correct kind of protein, the pros are that they are:

- a lot lower in fat than meat protein
- far more absorbable than meat or vegetable protein
- very convenient and filling.

What you should be looking for is either whey protein isolate or whey protein concentrate (being basically the only ingredient), egg albumen and casein. They are all *low in fat* and *high in protein*. It's important to read all the ingredients on the labels, because if the shakes contain sugars, full cream, vegetable or any other oil, give them a big *fat* miss! Those containing soy protein too high on the list of ingredients are selling you a little short of useful ingredients.

In Summary

Armed with the protein chart, you should be able to make the best choices every time, now knowing the importance of choosing wisely. One last thing to remember: it doesn't matter how fabulously high in amino acids and how absorbable or low in cholesterol the protein is if you cover it in fat when cooking it.

All meat should be unprocessed, ie fillets only. Cooking should be done without oil (including olive oil), butter, margarine, or cooking sprays. Use a non-stick pan, the grill and oven. Steam, char-grill, bake, dry-fry. Enjoy!

> Remember, think before you cook
> and think before you eat!

PROTEIN CHART

Lean Protein (Listed from best to worst)

Whey Protein Isolate or Whey Protein Concentrate (Protein Shake)

These are the best form of protein available at present. Although available as one of many ingredients in a few different types of protein powders, the best form is when it's basically the only ingredient. WPI or WPC is the most highly absorbable protein available and is less than 1% fat. It is convenient as you can mix it and take it to work, and mix it in cooking if you wish. It is also very inexpensive. The latest scientific evidence shows that whey protein concentrate can actually boost the body's immunity by up to 500%. It's a great natural appetite suppressant and contains properties which help speed the body's metabolism. But it's important to understand that WPI or WPC is not a meal replacement, or a protein replacement; it is a natural protein. Consider it as a piece of chicken, for example, and have it with a small salad for dinner.

However, it's most important that you do not confuse pure WPI or WPC with ion exchange or ionised whey protein. There are some protein supplements available which contain these supposedly 'high tech' ingredients, which unfortunately, in reality, have undergone a considerable amount of chemical treatment. This treatment removes much of the valuable calcium, as well as many of the other beneficial properties of pure WPI or WPC, including the immune boosting and cellular regeneration benefits. Pure WPI or WPC is NOT chemically treated, and the protein structure remains as nature intended it, ready for our bodies to be nourished by it. WPI is generally more expensive than WPC because it contains a higher amount of protein. These products are available in your local health food store.

Egg Albumen (Protein Shake)

This is another good form of protein. It is available in a powder mix and is fairly inexpensive. It is very absorbable and low in fat. It too is convenient, as you can mix it and take it with you to work; also you can use it in cooking if you wish.

Eggs

Eggs are a great form of protein – there is absolutely no cholesterol in the whites, which is what I recommend you eat most of. Never have more than one egg yolk per day. One egg yolk scrambled with four to six egg whites in an omelette is delicious. Simply mix with some vegies and use a non-stick frypan. Eggs are cheap and should be used often in your eating plan. In case you are wondering what to do with the unused yolks – throw them away or feed them to your cat!

White Fish

I'm referring to the fresh variety that is neither tuna nor salmon, nor any other seafood for that matter. White fish contain minimal amounts of fish oil, but more than enough for your daily fix, so you don't need to dip it in batter and fry it in oil. Check out my fish recipes in the Fat Free Recipes section (see p. 171).

Brown Fish

Brown fish is tuna and salmon, and any other type of fish which has dark flesh. It usually is a little more oily than white fish. It is, however, an excellent source of protein and is readily available – especially tinned tuna and salmon. Tuna contains the least amount of fat of the brown fish varieties. Remember, when selecting any tinned food, go for tuna in brine or spring water, not in oil. Some of the new varieties of tuna snacks available contain oil and mayonnaise, so be careful. Most of the tinned salmon is very oily, so purchase freshly filleted salmon when possible. Pink salmon is fractionally lower in fat than red salmon.

Turkey

Turkey doesn't have to be saved for Christmas dinner – it is lower in fat than chicken! The only problem is that it may be a little harder to find than chicken. You can substitute it for the chicken in any of the chicken recipes.

Chicken

Chicken seems to be most people's favourite form of protein. Chicken is easy to cook in different ways, and it's great to eat hot or cold. Make sure that you only eat chicken breast, as the thighs, legs and wings contain a higher fat content. Also, ensure all traces of skin, fat and gristle are removed *before* cooking. One of my favourite recipes is my Unfried Chicken Strips (see p. 181). Stay away from any processed chicken, such as chicken loaf. The way chicken is cooked will determine how much fat you end up eating, so save barbecued chicken for your Junk Day, and try to avoid fried chicken completely (if you can!).

Veal

When you're buying veal, make sure to ask your butcher if it is tender, and then ask him to trim off any fat. You will usually have to trim again at home, as most butchers don't think that 'that tiny bit of fat' will hurt you. We know it will! Cook it slowly and carefully. For some ideas, check out the Veal recipes (see p. 207).

Beef

Beef is high in protein, essential vitamins and minerals, including iron, but you do only need a small piece of it now and again. Include it in your weekly eating plan for variety and taste, but please limit it, because it's number nine on the list, which means there are eight other leaner, lower in fat types of protein to go for first.

Lamb

Lamb is quite high in fat, even when it's lean. It's only included here for a change of scenery. Lean filleted lamb is delicious marinaded with sweet chilli sauce and char-grilled. Have a look at the Roast Lamb with Rosemary (see p. 220). If you must have a roast dinner, at least try this fat free recipe!

Pork

Again, I've added pork here but only for variety. It is now available much leaner than in years gone by, but even in its new, lean form, it is really still too high in fat to eat on a regular basis. Only buy the pork fillets and make sure you go over the meat for any traces of fat before cooking.

Vegetables

If you are a vegetarian and you don't eat any dairy products or eggs, then your choice of protein is limited. A combination of vegetables will get you where you want to go, if it's your only choice, but just watch the fat content of what you're eating. You can combine green vegies with grains and rice, or mushrooms with green peas, brussel sprouts, broccoli and cauliflower, or soya beans with brown rice, wheat or corn. Remember though, *there is no protein in fruit*. I've included some appetising vegetarian recipes in the Fat Free Recipes section (see p. 232). However, if you are a vegetarian and you are able, do try to include whey protein and eggs in your daily eating plan.

Fatty Protein (Listed from bad to worst)

Grams of fat per 100 gram serving (in other words – % of fat)

Brawn	16.6	Lamb's fry with bacon	32.8
Devon	18.3	Salami	33.9
Chicken loaf	18.3	Pepperoni	36.0
Bacon (grilled)	19.2	Oxtail/Beef (average)	29.3
Soya beans (dry)	20.2	Spam	30.6
Haggis	21.5	Cabanossi	31.6
Sausages (thick)	21.3	Peanuts, dry roasted	47.6
Roast pork (2 slices)	26.7	Sunflower seeds	51.3
Lamb chump chop (fatty)	28.0	Pine nuts	71.0

> Fatty protein should be left out completely, including all kinds of processed meats, and many so-called health products!

CARBOHYDRATES

Carbohydrates (carbs) were thought to be fattening until not so long ago. The first thing a dieter would do is drop potatoes, pasta and bread completely from their diet. This, of course, left little of any substance to eat, and so left the poor dieter starving!

Then came the carbs revolution: 'They are okay.' The experts said they have little or no fat, and a new form of dieting was found. So then, why isn't everyone trim and taut as promised? After all, carbs don't have fats unless you add them, do they? Let's see why.

The main role of carbs in the body is as an energy source. Without them, you'd barely be able to do normal day-to-day tasks, let alone try to maintain a healthy exercise regime as well. The body specifically uses carbs when it's working anaerobically (without oxygen). For example, carbs are like fuel for the sweaty people, puffing and panting throughout a workout. Unfortunately, that's where the problem with carbs lies.

The modern dieter, who takes in plenty of low-fat carbs morning, noon and night, had better be busting a gut for hours on end to ensure all this excess fuel is burnt up. Otherwise *it will be stored as FAT!* Wouldn't you rather be busting your gut burning fat instead of carbs? (More later!)

One myth ripe for dispelling is that eating a lot of carbs will give you heaps of energy, as the advertisements for breakfast cereals would have us believe. Unless you are fit and toned, it's like putting premium fuel into an old car. It won't really add to the performance until the engine has been tuned. And, unlike the car, we get another top-up each day, so our fuel tanks have to expand to take all the excess.

There are several different carbs, but we are mainly concerned with *fibrous* and *starchy*.

Starchy carbs are digested much quicker than fibrous carbs (crunchy vegetables and bran) so they instil a higher concentration of energy into the blood. That's why you are told to eat a banana when playing sport. Unfortunately though, *if your body cannot burn the energy there and then, it stores it.*

Check out the following carbohydrate chart for the

different types of starchy and fibrous carbs. Although carb foods don't contain much fat, the body is easily able to convert them into fat for storage, if they are not used.

However, carbs do play a vital role in the *Fat Free Forever!* lifestyle:

- They reassure your body that you are not in a famine, and so stop your metabolism from slowing down.
- They fill you up.
- They contain vital vitamins and minerals.
- They help provide energy for good training and energetic living.
- They contain most of the roughage required in your diet.

As you can see, carbs are a powerful weapon for healthy living, but must be handled with a lot of thought and care.

The best way to enjoy the benefits of carbs has been explained in Body Types and Metabolism (see p. 42). If necessary, give it another read, so that it's clear.

Starchy and fibrous carbs are known as complex carbohydrates. A third carbohydrate is sugar carbs, known as simple carbohydrates. Simple carbohydrates are usually refined or processed food, as opposed to the more raw or unprocessed complex carbohydrates. They are digested very quickly into the system, and release large amounts of glucose into the body – hence the sugar rush from eating a chocolate bar.

> The problem with simple carbs is that you
> must burn them off with exercise,
> or else they will be stored!

Fibrous carbs are a vital part of any diet, as well as healthy living. Fortunately, fibrous carbs can be eaten all day, in filling amounts, thus aiding good internal health on your way to a great external shape.

Although in the carbohydrate chart I have referred to amounts of each starchy carbohydrate to eat each day, this is only a suggestion. You will be the best judge of what your body needs each day. If you find that your results are too slow, maybe it's time to cut back a little more on your starchy carb intake. It's impossible to prescribe exactly what you need, as everyone is different. You will become the best judge in time.

CARBOHYDRATES CHART

Starchy Carbohydrates (In no particular order)

> These are important in your daily eating plan.
> The amounts you eat and the time of day you eat
> them will help determine your body's shape.

Cereal

Your breakfast shouldn't be wasted on eating cardboard – no matter how low in fat the cardboard is! You should eat something which is high in fibre and filling, such as oats made with skim milk, or some other high fibre and low in fat and sugar cereal. If you have a favourite low-fat cereal which happens to be high in sugar, use it just as a topping over your more healthy cereal. Be careful: even though some cereals, including muesli, are 97–98% fat free, these figures are provided on a very small amount. You have to make choices which will help determine your body shape, so read the packets and be wary.

Pasta

Nearly everyone eats pasta. It can be enjoyed in many different ways – although for a great body shape, I suggest you steer away from traditional Italian dishes loaded with olive oil. Make up your own recipes, or check out the variety listed in the Fat Free Recipes section (see p. 171). Limit your intake of pasta though, as it does take a substantial amount of activity to use it all up. If pasta is part of your lunch, eat around one cup of cooked pasta, maximum. Pasta encompasses all different types of noodles, including instant. Be wary of the two minute noodles which are coated in oil. Go for the fat free variety instead.

Rice

Rice is easy to cook and is great with any meat or vegies. Although brown rice is fractionally higher in fat than white rice, it is a better choice. It has more fibre, is more difficult for your body to absorb, and more likely to be burned off. If you really cannot stand anything but white rice, then eat it. It's more important that you choose what you will actually stick to. There are some great fragrant rices on the market, such as jasmine. Remember, you don't need a lot for energy – a little will take you a long way. Don't forget, even rice noodles, although low in fat, are considered starchy carbohydrates.

Potatoes

You are probably thinking, 'What's dinner with no potatoes?' It's a better body shape – that's what it is! Although low in fat themselves, potatoes are starchy and stored easily by the body unless you are quite active. Jacket potatoes cooked in a hot oven without oil are great, or jammed with finely chopped vegies and strips of chargrilled chicken breast. Eat and enjoy them, but just make sure you limit them! If you were having them for your lunch, only have one medium-sized, or a couple of smaller-sized potatoes.

Bread

We've been told in recent times that bread is fine, it's just what you put on it that's potentially not! That's true enough, but too much bread can make a difference when you're trying hard to get into shape. Limit your bread intake to around two pieces per day. Go for the normal-sized bread, not the super-duper-can't-fit-in-the-toaster-sized bread. Wholegrain breads contain more fibre and, similarly to brown rice, are going to aid your metabolism speeding up. If you must eat white bread, go for the newer variety of white bread which is very high in fibre. Bread includes anything made of flour – muffins, scones, pastries, rolls, pancakes, pikelets, etc.

Fibrous Carbohydrates (Listed from best to worst)

Fruit

You can eat any fruit, but limit bananas as they are fairly high in sugars and carbs, and avocadoes, which although low in cholesterol, are really high in fat. You'd need to train like an Olympic athlete before burning them off! Eat a couple of pieces of fruit each day, but try not to have any at night, when your metabolism is working at its slowest. Stay away from fruit juices, even if they are 100% fruit, because they are very high in fruit sugars. A diluted glass once in a while is okay, but certainly not daily. Water is always your staple drink for a great body. Limit your intake of dried fruits because you tend to eat more of them. Certainly don't get caught thinking that dry mixes from the health food shop are going to be good for you. They are loaded with nuts, natural sugars and fat.

Vegetables

All vegies are great. When you know what your starchy carbs are, you will become more inventive with your fibrous carbs. Vegetables such as carrots, celery, cucumber, green beans and lettuce can literally be grazed on all day. When eaten with plenty of water throughout the day, they actually work as 'negative vegetables', meaning they burn more calories and fat than they contain themselves! They're excellent for snack attacks. Try to only lightly cook your vegies. The crunchier they are, the more fat they can help you burn. And don't cook them with any oil, not even cooking spray – ever!

FATS

There is no such thing as low-fat fat!

Fats are very misunderstood.

Like most other areas of nutrition, scientists discover something new about fats on a regular basis. However, we really need to be sure that we have the best information available with regards to fats, because what we do with them will make an *enormous* difference to our body's shape.

Let's look at the three types of fats.

Saturated Fats

Are really bad heart attack material. These are dripping, lard, butter, and vegetable oil.

Polyunsaturated Fats

Are low in cholesterol, and sold to make you feel good! They contain the same nine calories per gram as saturated fats. These are most margarines, even light, low, cholesterol free ones.

Monounsaturated Fats

Are sold as healthy, until you start trying to believe that you won't actually get fat from eating fat – *wrong*! They also contain the same nine calories per gram as saturated and polyunsaturated fats. These are olive oils.

What's Good about Fat?

The body needs fat for protection of its organs. It also needs fat as an energy source for aerobic activity. At this point, I'd like to explain the difference between aerobic and anaerobic activity, so you can better understand the fat-burning process.

Aerobic Activity

Believe it or not, aerobic activity is not jumping around in an aerobics class at your local gym, nearly killing yourself because of the lack of oxygen your body is suffering from. It is *steady* exercise, such as walking or cycling. As a result of taking part in steady aerobic exercise each day, *your body will burn fat.*

Anaerobic Activity

This is the type of activity that has caused many people to give up exercising completely. It should be left to the fitness fanatic. Most people are not fit enough to benefit from taking part in high-impact aerobics or boxercise classes. There will be more on this very interesting topic in the Exercise section (see p. 122). When you are breathless, your body is unable to burn fat, as it requires oxygen to do the job!

•

So, fat is fat, *or is it?* For the benefit of a better body, *yes it is.* For technical boffins, recent studies suggest that monounsaturated fats are slightly less likely to be stored directly as a fat cell than the dreaded killer, obese-making saturated fats.

> Beware of so-called 'healthy' foods
> containing saturated fats, such as vegetable
> or coconut oil.

To be healthy, it is important that your body contains some fat. But take a good look in the mirror. It probably looks as though your fat stores won't run out for a while! Having said that, if you have an eating disorder, or if you have a tendency to see yourself as fat when everyone around you tells you that you are not, be very careful. Reducing your calorie and fat intake when you are underweight can cause serious health problems. If you're unsure, ask your doctor.

Your Daily Menu Planner (see p. 98), which I am suggesting you follow, contains around 20 grams of unseen fat. By unseen fat, I mean fat in an egg yolk, fat in skim milk, fat in low-fat yoghurt, fat in really lean meat, and fat in fish oil, from fish. This minimal amount of unseen fat is plenty to live on, so don't be surprised when I say you should positively, absolutely, not add any more! This is what sets the *Fat Free Forever!* body shaping lifestyle apart from any other 'diet' around. Just a little more fat will hinder your progress.

If you eat 35 or 40 grams of fat in one meal (which is *easy* to do), for example, one serving of pasta carbonara, or half a family-sized block of dark chocolate, it will take up to one hour of solid aerobic walking (that's the steady, fat-burning pace), just to return to what you were before you ate it! Knowing how lethal fat is in the battle for a great body shape, it's my strongest hope and desire that you will just *leave it out*!

Fat fact   Most people have enough body fat to last them on a run from Sydney to Melbourne.

DAIRY PRODUCTS

Dairy products are in a category of their own because they contain a good mix of the three other categories: proteins, carbohydrates and fats. They can be the best in protein and the worst in fat!

So many people have given up dairy products because they believe doing so will make them healthy, and it seems almost trendy to do so at the moment. Lactose intolerance has become a catch phrase. Unfortunately, though, a great number of people are cutting out dairy products for *no real reason*.

> Low-fat dairy products can be your best friend in the fight against fat!

Low-fat dairy products are God's gift to a great body shape – and nothing short of! A low-fat, sugarless yoghurt can make your day much more bearable when you crave junk food, and can be eaten *any time of day*.

Because of the high-fat content of cheese, it's best avoided. Unless it is around 98–99% fat free, even the low-fat brands contain more than a desirable level of fat.

Always read labels carefully and if you must eat a cheese, choose wisely and eat in strict moderation.

Skim milk can be turned into a fruit smoothy delight. It too can be drunk *any time of day*. It is a great protein and very low in carbohydrate and fat.

If you don't particularly like the taste of the fresh skim milk available from your supermarket, try the UHT variety. It is full-bodied, tastes creamy and one of the best things about it is that you can buy a dozen at a time and store them.

If you feel that you are, or may be, lactose intolerant, try taking in small amounts of dairy products (with the okay from your doctor first, of course), as this may slowly stimulate the enzymes you need to tolerate lactose in your body. Alternatively, pineapple is a good enzyme to try.

One of the greatest benefits of consuming plenty of dairy products each day, especially for women, is the amount of calcium they supply. It's frightening to think about all the women who have cut out dairy products for fear that they would make them fat – or even more simply because they didn't like them. These women open themselves up to become dangerously deficient in calcium.

Chapter 7

Water and Other Drinks

Most of us are aware that we should drink water. Few people, however, realise how vitally important it is to our well-being. To give you some idea of how much water is contained in your body, have a look at these statistics:

Lungs: 90%
Blood: 82%
Brain: 76%
Bones: 25%

> Many people suffer from lethargy and tiredness in the afternoon. However, in nine out of ten cases, it's not sugar or carbohydrate energy that's lacking, it's the effects of dehydration.

Water is best absorbed by your body plain. Drinks such as tea, coffee and alcohol actually cause dehydration, so the more of these you drink, the more water you should consume. For example, for every cup of tea I drink, I try to have two extra cups of water on top of my daily water requirements.

What are the daily water requirements? Current wisdom says eight glasses a day – but how big is a glass? I am recommending that you drink at least one and a half litres of (preferably bottled or filtered) water each day. If you're not sure of this amount, keep a used drink bottle, wash it and refill it each morning.

You'll be surprised how easy it is when it becomes part of your daily routine. The more water you drink, the more thirsty for water you become.

Flavoured drinks can't be considered plain water, as flavoured liquids will often be digested differently. Add a squeeze of fresh lemon or lime juice if you need flavour. Remember, some flavoured drinks can dehydrate you, so be sure you reach your one and a half litre quota of plain water each day, minimum.

Tap water these days is far from beneficial to your health – especially if you are drinking several litres of it. The chemicals which are added to clean it are quite toxic, and too many of them can be cumulative.

> Your number one choice should be purified or distilled water.

A lot of mineral waters are as bad, or worse, than tap water, and can contain several chemicals – most of which are untreated. I'm not saying that it's going to make you ill, it's just that for optimum well-being and body function, wouldn't you prefer 80% of your body to consist of clean water, with minimum amounts of heavy metals, pesticides, chemicals and carcinogens?

Don't kid yourself that mineral water is going to provide any great amount of useful minerals. The content is so minute that to drink distilled water (the cleanest type) will make literally no difference to your daily mineral intake.

I had a water filter put into my sink at home some time ago, which has cut the expense of buying bottles and bottles and bottles of filtered water! There are less expensive methods of filtering water; check with your local health food shop for the most up-to-date product information.

> Sports drinks are *very* over-rated, and one of the big traps for body shapers.

Good intentions can lead to the consumption of several hundred calories you simply do not need. If you are overdoing getting fit, or training for an event, then a fluid replacer, or electrolyte, can help a lot. *But* if you are burning fat at optimum levels, then water is more than adequate for rehydration.

Alcohol is high in calories and is best kept for consumption in moderation for your Junk Day.

If you feel that you can't get enough energy for that early-morning walk, a good old faithful cup of coffee or tea (with skim milk) will serve well in giving you a boost, which also helps raise your metabolism without any excess fat or sugar. For a pick-me-up, diet colas are another form of caffeine which you can drink if you wish. I don't recommend that you go crazy with these drinks. Drink them sparingly. That way, they will work a lot better, as your body doesn't become accustomed to the artificial stimulation and artificial sweeteners.

Chapter 8

Vitamins

This can be a sensitive topic that people become very passionate about, especially with regards to their preferred vitamins. So often we've heard people say, 'I get all the vitamins I need from food'. The unfortunate reality is that this is extremely unlikely for the average person because of pollution, toxins, fast living, stress, lack of exercise, over-exercise, or simply because of the poor nutrients in the food most people eat.

Most processed, mass-produced food is treated, refined, stored, preserved, irradiated, frozen, force-fed, chemically enhanced, and/or grown in industrially polluted farm soils with cheap, nutritionally empty fertilisers that produce a lot of empty, water-filled produce.

Sounds appetising, doesn't it? Just one of these factors is more than enough to totally ruin the nutritional quality of food, and if it doesn't, there is always the way we cook and store the food at home that will really finish off the job!

The Government's Recommended Daily Allowance

(RDA) is based on data designed to provide the minimum amount of a nutrient needed to prevent certain diseases, such as scurvy. It was initially established for the average person from a time when life was less stressful. The minimum requirement isn't able to diagnose any of your individual vitamin requirements, to know the quality of the food you eat, or how your particular body assimilates food.

This information may appear critical, and certainly is open to controversy, but the average diet doesn't hold much nutrition at all, and a dieting diet usually contains even less.

Although throughout Your Daily Menu Planner (see p. 98) and Fat Free Recipes it is suggested that you eat plenty of fresh fruit, vegetables, dairy products and lean meats, it's important to realise that even the freshest of foods are often subject to inadequate growing, storage and handling these days.

So, to prevent illness and to ensure maximum health and performance of your body (and that includes your ability to burn fat and shape up), I suggest a few simple vitamins to include daily.

VITAMIN C

Vitamin C is vital for the production of collagen, which is the cement which binds just about your whole body. It helps to build the immune system and protects against antioxidants which cause old age, as well as helping to repair the body after a hard day. The minimum amount taken per day should be 1000 to 2000 mg. An orange contains 10 mg of vitamin C, so you can see how many of them you'd have to eat! If you feel run down or as though you may be coming down with something, double the dose, or even treble it. It's important that you take vitamin C *before* you get sick, as it works far better as a preventative medicine than it does a cure.

VITAMIN B COMPLEX

Vitamin B complex is the commando of the B group of vitamins. It's great against stress. If you're feeling run down, take one or two each day, depending on the type and what the bottle label says.

MULTIVITAMINS

It is very important to purchase a good-quality multi-vitamin. A lot of vitamins can be bought quite cheaply, but what most people don't realise is that in the case of vitamins you really do get what you pay for. The cheaper vitamins are usually the least absorbable and in really low doses, so you need to take more. Go for quality, as this ensures that you are not missing anything important in your diet. Ask at your local health food shop or chemist if you aren't sure about what's best for you.

CALCIUM

I hope by now most people are aware of the absolute importance of calcium, especially women. Unfortunately, most women, and nearly as many men, are calcium deficient, and don't even make the minimum RDA! The so-called calcium-rich dairy products contain calcium that is only about 20% absorbable.

The 800 mg RDA that you think you are getting from your two glasses of full-cream milk is only giving you 170–200 mg of useable calcium, which leaves you 600 mg short of the RDA. As you can see, good supplements can be useful. Again, be aware that many calcium supplements are not well absorbed and therefore are a waste of money. Calcium carbonate is the most absorbable.

IRON

A great many women have found that they are iron deficient. This is another example of poor modern living. An iron supplement is a lot lower in fat than a piece of lean red meat, although eating a steak once a week is not a bad thing. Iron is responsible for carrying oxygen in the blood, so you can see that since the brain and muscles need oxygen to work, iron is vital. Coffee and tea can actually block the absorption, so this is another great reason to supplement your iron intake.

Chapter

9

Timing Your Meals

Your body's energy levels vary throughout the day. Rather than depriving your body of necessary foods that may be considered heavy, such as starchy carbohydrates, following is a schedule which enables you to eat plenty of nutritious foods, it's just that they're probably in a different order to what has been normal for you.

This is an area of habit replacement which will prove vital to improving your body's shape. Making correct choices will give you the results you're after.

> You can't talk your way out of problems you've behaved yourself into.
> Stephen R. Covey

In the following pages of Your Daily Menu Planner, you'll see that at the top of each page is a box containing essential information on the type of food you should be eating at that meal and the time of day you should eat it.

It's important to understand that Your Daily Menu Planner has been designed to help you, so use my guidelines, but feel free to adapt them to your lifestyle. So you know the boundaries: you cannot change the type of food to eat at each meal, but you can change the timings within a half-hour flexibility radius.

This means that if it's 11.30 am and you haven't had your mid-morning snack, then make sure you still eat it – but have it before noon. Then, because you're running a little late, have your lunch at the later end of the scale, and get back on track ready for your afternoon snack.

Once you learn this lifestyle, it's easy. Your body actually does the learning and remembering for you. It will let you know that it needs a meal or a snack, and when you check your watch, you'll realise that it always lets you know right on time.

Chapter 10

Your Daily Menu Planner

The different foods listed on the following pages are simply suggestions that have worked well for me. If you can find suitable alternatives, go right ahead, but remember to watch the fat content of anything you include. Keep the amounts medium-sized at first. If you feel you're not getting the results fast enough, cut back a little. If you feel as though you could eat a horse at the end of the day, then increase a little. It's important to find your own balance – it's a personal thing.

When you are cooking, use either non-stick pans or good quality stainless steel pans, and *never* use cooking sprays. They are *FAT*! And remember: don't add butter, margarine, mayonnaise, cream, oil or sugar. And watch the amount of starchy carbs you eat each day.

BREAKFAST

> Eat a medium serving of Starchy Carbohydrates
> between 5 and 9 am

1½ cups cereal, high in fibre, low in fat, low in sugar, with
1 cup of skim milk and
¼ cup fruit and
2 tablespoons low-fat yoghurt and
1 dessertspoon honey

Start with 300 mL of water, then you can have tea or coffee with your breakfast. Don't drink any fruit juice as it's high in sugar.

You will not necessarily feel really full after eating this meal. Your mid-morning snack is just around the corner, so pace yourself and you will be full enough in time. Breakfast kick-starts your metabolism for the day and will help in burning fat and raising blood-sugar levels, increasing your general energy.

MID-MORNING SNACK

Eat a small serving of Protein with a very small serving of Fibrous and/or Starchy Carbohydrates between 9 and 11.30 am

> 3 eggs (3 whites, 1 yolk), scrambled without butter, served on 1 piece of unbuttered toast
> *or* 200 grams low-fat flavoured yoghurt with 2 plain rice cakes

Drink 300 mL water first, then you can have tea or coffee with your snack. If you like, you can have a diet soft drink instead of the tea or coffee, but *not* instead of the water, and preferably not every day!

After a couple of days, you will crave this snack. It's part of breakfast and part of lunch. It puts you into grazing mode, which keeps your metabolism on fire, and this helps again in burning fat. The most amazing part of this snack is that if you miss it, by 5 or 6 pm, you will know it! If you have cravings at that time of day, which is normal for most people, it's because you have missed this snack, or your afternoon snack.

LUNCH

> Eat a medium serving of Protein with a medium serving of Starchy and Fibrous Carbohydrates between 11.30 am and 1.30 pm

1½ cups cooked brown rice with
150 grams tuna in brine or char-grilled chicken breast and a squeeze of lime juice and soy sauce

or 1 sandwich containing chicken breast and salad with no butter or cheese and only fat free mayonnaise

or choose a pasta or potato dish from the Fat Free Recipes section (see p. 171).

Drink 300 mL water first, then eat.

Your lunch will become the focus of your day, just as your dinner has been in the past, as it is now the main meal of the day. Make the absolute most of this meal, because for the rest of the day the meals become smaller and smaller!

AFTERNOON SNACK

Eat a small serving of Protein with a very
small serving of Starchy and/or Fibrous
Carbohydrates between 1.30 and 3 pm

200 grams low-fat flavoured yoghurt with
an apple or pear
or 250 mL protein shake with
2 plain rice cakes (if you didn't have them earlier)

Drink 300 mL water first, then you can have tea or coffee with your snack, or a diet soft drink instead of the tea or coffee – not instead of the water, and preferably not every day.

Again, after a couple of days, you will actually crave this meal. It's part of lunch and part of dinner, in the grazing mode. If you miss this important meal, you will definitely feel it around 6 to 8 pm!

STOP!

HOLD IT RIGHT HERE!

PLEASE READ THIS
BEFORE YOU GO ANY FURTHER

Because your body's metabolism slows down later in the day so you can sleep at night, the later in the day you eat, the more careful you must become in your selection of food.

To help you, dinner has been split into two sections, depending on whether you eat early *or* late.

> **Remember that it's *either* early *or* late dinner, *not both*!**

EARLY DINNER

> Eat a medium serving of Protein with a small
> serving of Fibrous Carbohydrates
> (no starchy carbs!) between 3 and 7.30 pm

> 150 grams fish or chicken breast cooked without oil,
> with
> 1½ cups lightly-steamed vegetables or green salad
> a squeeze of lime juice and fat free salad dressing
> *or* 500 mL protein shake, with
> a crunchy salad with fat free dressing, followed by
> 200 grams low fat yoghurt

Drink 300 mL water first, then eat. You can then have a cup of tea or coffee afterwards.

The earlier you eat this meal the better. For absolutely optimum results in the shortest amount of time (without cheating), have the protein shake and salad for dinner each night, whether it's early or late. Try it and see how you go. Have a break for a couple of weeks and try it again. You will *definitely* like the results! Ensure you go for variety, and don't let yourself become bored! Save the dessert recipes listed in the Fat Free Recipes section (see p. 171) for Junk Day.

LATE DINNER

> Eat a medium serving of Protein ONLY between
> 7.30 and 10 pm

       500 mL protein shake followed by
       200 grams low-fat yoghurt
  or 4 eggs (1 yolk only), scrambled without butter, with
       a sprinkle of seasoning sauce on top (no toast)
       followed by
       200 grams low-fat yoghurt

Drink 300 mL water first, then eat. You can then have a cup of tea or coffee afterwards.

What you eat for this meal is crucial. Again, for absolutely optimum results in the shortest amount of time (without cheating), have the protein shake as your first choice. The great thing with the protein shake is that you can mix it in the morning and take it with you if you are going to be out late – and you don't have to think twice about what to eat for this important meal.

If you're prone to the midnight munchies, relax – this will go away. Try a small glass of skim milk instead, until your body gets used to your new routine.

Chapter 11

Junk Day!

THE DAY YOU'VE BEEN WAITING FOR

For being so very good and sticking with the *Fat Free Forever!* body shaping lifestyle, you can have one junk day each week – maximum. This means you can have anything from pizza to pasta with cream, or fried chicken and a chocolate sundae.

One tip though: try to keep it to one meal per week, rather than all day, for the best results! ENJOY!!

WHAT IS JUNK DAY?

With all the hard work that goes with a more healthy eating lifestyle, I've provided you with some release. It's JUNK DAY, one day per week. Having a Junk Day each week not only keeps you sane and makes the days in each week pass quickly for you, but it actually aids in speeding up your metabolism.

The body doesn't know what's happening when you eat fat after not eating it all week, so your metabolism goes into overdrive. It works in your favour to have a junk day once a week, providing, of course, you go straight back to the *Fat Free Forever!* lifestyle the next day!

There's obviously varying degrees of damage you can do on your Junk Day. That's why I've listed a Bad to Worst chart of food you can eat on Junk Day, to help you make somewhat healthier choices – if you want. You will find that you don't have to go all out to become satisfied. A little goes a long way, especially when your body is *not* used to eating junk anymore!

When you reach your body shaping goal, you will be able to have more than one Junk Day a week, without making any difference to your body shape. That's the benefit of having a faster metabolism and learning to live a disciplined lifestyle – *forever!*

> You should ENJOY your Junk Day!
> Absolutely guilt free!

JUNK FOOD CHART
(Listed from bad to worst)

	grams of fat per serve	calories per serve
Barbecued chicken (no skin)	8	190
Tasty cheese (30g)	10	120
Toasted muesli (60g)	11	267
Ice-cream, regular (1 scoop)	11	165
Milk chocolate (small block)	14	263
Pizza (single slice)	15	340
Fruit muffin	16	296
Beef curry	17	344
Cheesecake (100g)	19	315
Thai noodles (100g)	20	285
Regular-sized french fries	20	329
Hot dog	20	370
Sausage roll	22	378
Lasagne	24	546
Avocado dip (quarter cup)	24	250

JUNK FOOD CHART *(Continued)*
(Listed from bad to worst)

	grams of fat per serve	calories per serve
Quiche Lorraine	25	360
Fish and chips	28	500
Pork ribs	30	400
Spinach and cheese filo triangle (large)	30	400
Fried chicken (2 pieces)	30	410+
Meat pie	30	500
Hamburger (with the lot)	30	500+
Cadbury's Dairy Milk Chocolate (100g)	30	525
Toblerone (100g)	31	544
Banana split with cream and ice-cream	32	600
Poppy seeds (half-cup)	33	338
Flaky pastry (100g)	37	556
Chocolate-coated almonds (12–14 nuts)	44	568
Butter/Margarine (62.5g)	50	450
Eggs Benedict (2 eggs)	53	700

Chapter 12

Fat Free Food Flavourings

If oil didn't exist, you wouldn't be able to use it. The same goes for cream, butter, margarine and mayonnaise. Life may be completely boring without such a wonderful variety of fattening flavours, but they *are* fattening flavours, and should be put into a separate category, away from the flavours you will use in everyday life.

Your supermarket shelves are full of wonderful fattening flavour alternatives. Check the labels to see which are lowest in fat – then use your tastebuds as the ultimate test. You know what the boundaries are, so just work within them.

The main essentials are: non-stick cookware or good quality stainless steel cookware, a grill, oven and microwave. Without these, it's too tempting to use a little oil or spray so the food doesn't stick. The other important skill you will learn, besides sifting out the flavours with oil from the flavours without, will be timing your cooking. Cooking without any oil or cooking spray can be tricky at first. Once you get used to it, it's pretty easy. You have to be careful not to dry food out, and you will also become quite skilled at splashing in a little water, just to help food go golden, without letting it go soggy. It will become an art form for you, as it has for me. Over time and through experimenting, you will get better at fat free cooking.

I want to encourage you to be as creative as possible when it comes to the flavour and colour of the foods you eat. This is a major key in the *Fat Free Forever!* lifestyle.

There are very few recipes that I haven't been able to completely replicate in taste, texture and looks. There are some that I simply cannot, but to help you overcome the whole taste issue, if that's important to you, simply say to yourself, 'Oil doesn't exist – it's not an option any-more', and then prepare and cook accordingly. You must realise that if it's not *exactly* the same as it is with olive oil, then that's purely a choice issue – that only you can make.

> Don't let the tastebuds on your tongue determine the big bumps on your bum!

FAT FREE FOOD FLAVOURINGS CHART

> Remember, no fat, oil, butter, margarine, cream, and very limited sugar.

salt
pepper
all herbs (fresh/dry)
all spices
mustard (no added fat)
soy sauce
teriyaki sauce
Worcestershire sauce
fat free chilli sauce
garlic
ginger
oyster sauce
fat free tinned soups
French onion soup mix

tomato paste and puree
vinegar (any kind)
fat free salad dressings
honey
low-joule dessert toppings
small amounts of artificial
    sweeteners
lime and lemon juice
fat free stocks: liquid and
    powdered (chicken, beef,
    vegetable)
any other fat free flavours –
    read the ingredients label!

Chapter 13

Fat Free Shopping

Most people these days are careful shoppers when it comes to keeping within their financial budget, but don't have a clue about how to keep within a body shaping budget! The *Fat Free Forever!* lifestyle includes plenty of fresh, healthy and nutritious foods. Most processed foods can be classified unhealthy, as they're very high in fat, so they're automatically eliminated from the shopping list, to be replaced by fresh, natural foods.

Remember, anything marked 'light' or 'low' can be light and/or low in colour, texture, taste, cholesterol and everything else except fat! Some foods marked 'low fat' are required by law to be only 25% less than the regular food. So please be careful.

FAT FREE SHOPPING LIST

Everything should be available in your supermarket, or I've listed where else to look. Remember to watch the fat content of everything!

UHT skim milk

eggs

fat free flavoured yoghurts

whey protein isolate or whey protein concentrate powder (visit your health food store)

low fat, high-fibre, low sugar cereal

fat free seasoning sauces

fat free oyster sauce

fat free teriyaki sauce

fat free sweet chilli sauce

fat free salsa

100% fruit jams – no sugar or artificial sweeteners added

fat free rice cakes

a selection of starchy carbohydrates

fresh lean meat

fresh fruit and vegetables, including fresh herbs

water

any other foods and flavourings listed in the Fat Free Food Flavourings chart (see p. 112)

Chapter 14

Food FAQ

WHAT ABOUT CELLULITE?

Cellulite is fatty deposits in the body, and not toxins blocking fat, or anything else. The only way to get rid of cellulite is to get rid of the fat, by eating properly and exercising. You can do this by following the *Fat Free Forever!* body shaping lifestyle. It all comes down to what you eat, when you eat it, and how much exercise you do. There is no magic lotion or potion to eliminate cellulite. I had it, and I got rid of it by following the fat free lifestyle.

WHAT ABOUT SUGAR?

I'm sure by now you're wondering why I have hardly mentioned sugar. It's mainly because it's not a big issue.

That's not to say that you should eat large amounts of it, but fat is a far greater body shaping enemy. Although sugar does not contain fat, if it's not burned it will be stored as fat, so use it in moderation. Don't have it in your tea and coffee, but don't worry about it if it's in sauces in small amounts. Sugar substitutes such as artificial sweeteners or honey are alternatives, but eat them in moderation as well. Be careful you read the labels on everything. Sugar and fat together can be a disastrous body shaping combination!

WHAT ABOUT SALT?

Salt won't make you fat or thin, so decide on taste. I'm not preaching health here, just body shaping. Because it contains no calories, and of course no fat, salt is helpful to use in cooking. If you have high blood pressure or some other condition so that your doctor has limited your salt intake – then listen to your doctor. When you are using salt, always add it in moderation.

WHAT ABOUT CHOCOLATE?

As you will read in the Junk Food Chart (see p. 108), chocolate is way up there with the worst of them. This is mainly because of its fat rather than sugar content. Don't be fooled – carob is just as bad. So, save it for Junk Day. One tip though: if you have a sweet tooth and crave something, go for a couple of jubes or jelly beans instead of chocolate; at least they don't contain fat. If you are really craving sugar, especially later in the day, this is usually because you haven't eaten enough carbs earlier. There are a few really good, low-fat (97–98% fat free) chocolate ice-creams on the market. Limit these, as you will tend to overeat their recommended serving size, which means you'll end up eating loads more grams of fat than you thought.

WHAT ABOUT PREGNANCY?

It's really important that you don't do anything radical when pregnant. Take it from someone who knows. You need to eat plenty of fresh foods, but there is absolutely no reason why you shouldn't follow the *Fat Free Forever!* lifestyle. I did (most of the time!), and I gave birth to healthy-sized twins. The main point to remember is that you are the best and only judge of the amount of food you need. Just stick with the principles. I found it incredibly hard to exercise throughout my pregnancy, but I do recommend you try to walk every day. You'll need this added energy when Junior comes along – believe me!

WHAT ABOUT BREASTFEEDING?

Even the head lactation consultant at the hospital advised me that I only needed to drink water to produce breast milk. Providing you are eating plenty of dairy products (low-fat, of course), and lots of fresh fruit, vegetables, grains, eggs and lean meat, not only will your doctor be satisfied with what you're doing, but you and your baby will be too. Just keep coming back to the principles of the *Fat Free Forever!* lifestyle. I found that I didn't lose much of my weight during breastfeeding – it seemed to pour off a few months afterwards. I attribute this to being careful throughout the pregnancy and feeding periods, then working at it strictly for a few months.

WHEN IS THE BEST TIME FOR JUNK DAY?

This is a personal thing, depending on your lifestyle. I enjoy having my junk day on the weekend, so I can enjoy my time off. If you find that because of circumstances, you need to have two junk days in one week, then just be extra careful for the following ten days or so. You know the principles and you know the balance. On Sundays, I come home from church and enjoy having lunch with my family, and I just eat whatever I like! If you have a choice, it's better to have junk for lunch instead of dinner. At least then, your body has the rest of the afternoon to metabolize it, well before you go to sleep at night. Number one rule though, ENJOY your junk day!

WHEN CAN I EAT FAT AGAIN?

You will find that after you've been living the *Fat Free Forever!* lifestyle for a few weeks, it will be much easier to live without added fats in your diet. After a while your junk days will probably become healthier than the food you're eating currently. Your body won't crave fat, and you'll find that when you do eat it, it makes you feel sluggish and ill.

HOW MANY LOW CALORIE DRINKS CAN I HAVE EACH DAY?

This depends entirely on you. Water and milk are the only fluids you need, so anything above and beyond them is a matter of choice. Some diet drinks can dehydrate you, so ensure you drink enough water to compensate for them. Again, we're not talking about 'health' here, but we are talking about body shaping, so if, for the time being, drinking a diet soft drink will stop you from eating a bar of chocolate – go for it! Just have these types of drinks in moderation. A great alternative is fresh water with a squeeze of fresh citrus juice.

Chapter 15

Fat Free Recipe Guide

I have included one hundred great Fat Free Recipes towards the back of this book, starting on p. 171. These recipes have evolved over a number of years. As I've mentioned before, it's important that you increase the amount of variety in your diet, and you will then be less likely to think about food as a major issue. To help you do this, I've included plenty of variety, but by all means, add some flavours of your own. Never say never when it comes to transforming FAT to *Fat Free*. Just put your mind and tastebuds to the test, and give it a go. Once you've mastered the *Fat Free Forever!* lifestyle, tempt your palate and imagination further with the *Fat Free Forever Cookbook*, available now.

Before discovering the wonderful taste sensations found in the Fat Free Recipe section, enjoy reading Stage 3 on EXERCISE, which is *paramount* to your body shaping success.

Stage

3

Exercise

Chapter 16

Shape That Body!

Exercise is something you simply cannot avoid if you want to fully achieve your body shaping dreams. I can say it fast if it helps, or even whisper it, but you cannot ignore it. You need to exercise. It's a no-go zone for some and a life-saving love for others. Although sitting is better than lying down, and standing is better than sitting, walking is much better than standing, but running is *not* better than walking (unless, of course, you're really fit). Confused? Read on.

Let's explore the reasons why anyone should bother with exercise if they are getting good results from the *Fat Free Forever!* lifestyle without moving a muscle (which will happen).

Your body's ability to burn fat is very much dependent on the tone of your muscles. If they are strong and well-toned, you will be a far more efficient fat-munching machine. Now, I don't know about you, but if doing a little exercise will make the whole body shaping thing a little easier, I for one am going to do it. By taking part in some focused exercise, you can consume more foods that you enjoy, and at the same time turn even your everyday movements into efficient, fat-burning activities (mini workouts without you even realising that you're exercising).

> How you feel plays a large part in how you look.

Already, by following the *Fat Free Forever!* lifestyle, you will notice that you are sleeping better, and that you have more energy. This is great, but there's more! I'm sure you'll agree, if something makes you feel and perform better than you were previously, it's going to be a pleasure to continue it and make it a routine part of your life. Exercise releases hormones called endorphins which are responsible for your body's feeling of well-being. If done correctly, the right type of exercise will help your body to increase its ability to produce these natural feel-good hormones, and therefore also increase your ability to cope with stress, worry, or just twenty-first century living!

Although *Fat Free Forever!* is primarily a way of life that will ensure you have a better body shape, it also has another very positive side-effect – great health! Unfortunately, most methods used to change body shapes have detrimental effects on the body's health, especially in the long term. This lifestyle does just the opposite. And, if you include some body shaping exercise in your new lifestyle, you are increasing the value of the body shaping 'insurance policy' you have just taken out by reading this book. It is literally a deposit, in your favour, in the body shaping bank! Regular muscular stimulation is the only way, apart from good nutrition, to ensure maximum health, mobility and youthfulness as you age.

> 'Use it or lose it'
> One of the most important clichés ever quoted.
> Ignore it at your own risk!

So, what does it take? First of all, it's vital that you understand what exercise is before you can take part in it properly. You may have had quite extensive contact with various types of gym exercise, such as aerobics, pump, jump, thump, step, boxercise, Tai-Bo and circuit classes, or sports such as running, swimming, tennis or netball. You probably undertook this type of exercise with many good intentions, but more often than not, without the results which were promised or expected. Some of you may say it's your own fault for not being diligent enough, but it's usually true that it's just that you weren't doing the correct type of exercise to benefit a great body shape.

> Doing 50% of the right kind of exercise is far better than doing 100% of the wrong kind.

If you enjoy playing tennis, squash, netball or basketball, by all means, keep playing. But if you think it's all you need to get in shape, think again. Body shaping is definitely not a hit-and-miss thing. You can't just dip your hand into a big bag of activities and hope to achieve your goals by your good intentions, and a bit of sweat and luck to boot! If you consider body shaping a sport, then it may be easier to understand. Just as great jockeys don't play basketball to win the Melbourne Cup, and tennis players don't surf to win Wimbledon, it's important for you to understand that to achieve a better body shape, you have to train like a body shaper.

Have you ever seen a fat or podgy aerobics instructor? Every gym has at least one. Now why is it that these instructors, who take far more high-energy classes than you each week, are still overweight? Because they're usually eating wrong – overloading on carbs – to the extent that even the several aerobics classes each week can't shift the fat. Can you see the equation here? High-impact aerobics classes just do not equal fat loss and better body shape.

And it's not just aerobics classes which shake the equation. Add to it running, jogging, circuit classes and any other high energy activity. Why? Fat is a slow-burning energy. It is converted very slowly for use as a steady, long-lasting energy source.

Fat must have oxygen to allow it to burn in the same way as a flame needs oxygen.

High-energy, high-impact activities demand a fast supply of fuel to keep them going. They also need a fuel that doesn't rely on oxygen: chances are you will be out of breath (in oxygen debt), so at these times the body will choose one of its fast energy providers, such as carbohydrates or glycogen energy. Therefore, little or no fat is burnt by doing these types of activities.

'Oh, no!', I hear you groan. Wasted years jumping around for nothing. Well, not entirely.

Your fitness level will have improved and you will have toned certain muscles to some degree. You will also have stimulated your metabolism to work a little faster, but as I mentioned earlier, you should now be only interested in the 100% optimum most efficient ways to get in shape, so please, don't knock yourself out wasting any more time!

Chapter 17

Start Today!

Have you ever wondered why exercise is so hard? If your answer is 'yes', you are not alone. I spent years pondering this same question, and in my endeavours to find a shortcut to the whole aerobics and gym scenario, I discovered the answer to the dilemma. Training my mind. The main reason exercise is hard and not easy for many people is because they don't know how the body works and exactly what is needed to obtain a healthy and toned body shape.

> It is positively, absolutely, without any shadow of doubt, completely possible for you to have muscle tone where you'd never dreamt it possible.

I love and believe in people, and I am aware of the pain that people go through with regards to how they feel and look. I want to see you set completely free.

> Just remember,
> you don't have to be the best that
> Cindy Crawford, Elle McPherson or Kate Moss
> can be. THAT'S THEIR JOB,
> *not yours!*

It doesn't matter what age you are, or what stage you're at physically. You should be – *we all should be –* ready to become more active. And there is no better time than right now to say YES, instead of the usual, 'I'm starting back at the gym on Monday' routine! (You no doubt know what I mean!)

> 'Starting on a Monday'
> holds about as much promise as your last
> New Year's Resolution.

Why not start on a Tuesday! Monday is the most tried and failed day of the week to start a new exercise plan.

Although most people can afford to become much more active, there is a small group of people who fall into the exceptional 'over-exercising' category; they enjoy doing torturously difficult exercise just for the sake of it. If that's you, my advice would be *slow down*, and take a good look at why you do what you do!

It's my aim to turn the technical difficulties into body shaping simplicities. Unless you are an elite athlete or professional sports person, you really should be able to take part in some body shaping exercise, with great results.

Making time for exercise is important. Sometimes being busy is deceiving, and not necessarily constructive. We can be so busy with things that eat away at our time, without even being fully aware of them. Especially when you have a family.

> Something has to give way somewhere, and it's usually our health.

Looking after yourself may be a sacrifice. If you don't have time to exercise, then you have to choose to create some time, by giving your well-being some priority over other things or tasks.

For some people, it's a matter of life or death! It's pointless to be concerned about making money and spending more time with your family if you are going to kill yourself with a heart attack because of a poor diet and lack of exercise. Let's be realistic about what's REALLY important and what's not. You have to be around to enjoy your family and spend your money. So let's do something about that!

To ensure that I walk for an hour, five days a week, I have to wake up at 5.30 am. If I didn't, my next opportunity would be 11 pm at night!

Statistics show that 75% of people who say they will exercise in the morning actually do, and only 25% of people who say they will exercise in the evening actually do. This is enough reason to aim for the morning. If something has to go at the end of a busy day, it's usually exercise. Bring it to the beginning of your day, and watch it change your life – *for the better*.

> One of the requirements of a leader is energy.
> J. Oswald Sanders

If we are going to live a high-energy lifestyle, then we have to *sow* high-energy.

The answer to having more energy is not having more sleep or even having more rest. A recent survey found that 95% of people in the western world look forward to their weekends, but 52% of them feel more tired after their weekend than before.

If we want to maximise our potential in life, we need to live a high-energy lifestyle.

Have you ever thought that you'd like to feel less tired and be able to achieve more?

> Sow sparingly and you will reap sparingly.
> Sow abundantly and you will reap abundantly.
> Corinthians

If you want a high-energy life, you need to sow energy to reap it. The more you expend energy, the more energy you will have. Guaranteed! The more energy you try to conserve, the less energy you will have. Guaranteed! Remember, you reap what you sow.

Healthy exercise = abundant energy.

No exercise = next to no energy.

You choose!

When you exercise, don't think about how much energy you are expending – instead think about how much energy you will reap as a result of the energy you sow. It's worth it!

Chapter 18

Fat Burning

Walking is probably the best fat-burning method known. It's also the easiest and least likely to cause injury, so use it. Cycling is also good. The trick is to keep a good pace (not breathing hard) for as long as possible. This will guarantee you are burning fat. If you measure your heart rate, use the following formula to determine if you are exercising at the best pace.

> 220 minus your age = a
>
> 60–70% of a = b
>
> 'b' is your maximum heart rate per minute for burning fat.

What's best about fat burning is that it can be done almost any time, anywhere, from a walk to and from work, or parking the car a little further from the office, or pushing your baby around the park. So do try and find thirty minutes or more each day, to make a big difference to your results (see Body Shaping Exercise Chart p. 165).

> A brisk dawn or dusk walk clears away the cobwebs and helps you think.

With fat burning taken care of, let's now deal with another issue. I'm not going to give you a pile of regular bum, tum and thigh exercises. They are probably why you've bought this book – because they haven't worked for you! It's not just the exercise you do, but it is, more importantly, how you do them.

I have absolutely no objection to any sport or current exercise programme you may already enjoy. Keep it up if it's having the desired effect, that is, if it's increasing your fitness level, if your social or competitive needs are met, and if it is important to you. Basically, do it for pleasure, if you wish.

FAT LOSS CALCULATOR

TOTAL KILOS OF FAT LOSS POSSIBLE

Calories burned per day	1 month	2 months	3 months	4 months	5 months	6 months
50	0.2	0.4	0.6	0.8	1	1.2
100	0.4	0.8	1.2	1.6	2	2.4
150	0.6	1.2	1.8	2.4	3	3.6
200	0.8	1.6	2.4	3.2	4	4.8
250	1	2	3	4	5	6
300	1.2	2.4	3.6	4.8	6	7.2
350	1.4	2.8	4.2	5.6	7	8.4
400	1.6	3.2	4.8	6.4	8	9.7
450	1.8	3.63	5.4	7.2	9	10.9
500	2	4	6	8	10	12

Chapter 19

Walking

Walking is definitely my number one choice for those who want to lose weight, and you don't need training to learn how to do it!

My two best walking buddies over the past few years have been my dad and my sister Kathy. The only way I can fit my walk in each day is by being up and ready to go at 5.30 am. By the time I arrive home, my husband and kids are still asleep, so my routine doesn't affect theirs.

> How badly do you want to lose fat?
> Get up and get moving – NOW!

WHEN TO WALK?

I find the best time of day is 5.30 am, to ensure that I am able to fit everything else into my busy schedule. There are also very good metabolic reasons for walking first thing in the morning. It actually gives your metabolism a kick-start for the day, which means *fat burning*! Winter is a little more difficult as all is dark outside early in the morning – but just think, you'll be home in time to see the sun rise!

If you have decided to exercise each day, by doing it in the morning you are not only making it a priority, but you are basically getting it out of the way so you can focus on everything else. Otherwise, if you decide to walk in the evening, but run out of time, you will go to bed feeling like a failure, and that's extra pressure you do not need.

It would be good for you to walk in the morning, if you can. If not, it would be good for you to walk ... *full stop*!

WHERE TO WALK?

I choose to walk in one of the parks near where I live. It's great because one lap is 1.2 kilometres in total, including one really awesome hill, and a couple of good sized stretches of incline. It doesn't matter really where you choose to walk, but remember to keep the scenery as varied as possible, so you don't become bored.

Safety is also an issue.

If you walk alone, it's important to take care, and it would be better for you not to walk alone in the evening. I know in the park where I walk, there are many people out and about doing their 'thing' at 6 am, so it's a good safe place to be, and, of course, I have someone to walk with too!

There are other alternatives, such as walking in a low impact aerobic class. Just be sure that your heart rate remains consistent and that you are moving for at least 45 minutes. This is the best *fat burning* time.

Another alternative is walking the treadmill at the gym, or if you can afford it, walking the treadmill at home. It this suits you best because of safety and looking after kids, then go for it. The main thing is that you are able to walk somehow, some way. Walk where you won't be distracted, and walk where you have some good hills to help increase your fitness levels.

WHAT PACE AND FOR HOW LONG?

There's walking and there's WALKING. When I talk about walking, be assured, I'm talking about WALKING! This is at a considerable pace. Shoulders back, head up, walking at around 110–120 beats per minute. You should be able to hold a light conversation, but not be able to sing!

When you're walking, you should be breathing primarily through your nose and not your mouth, ie breathe normally! And, although you are feeling puffed, be assured that in a week or so your fitness levels will increase and increase. Basically you can only get fitter!

Now – the 3 x 20 theory which we hear so much about. It's on the TV helping to advertise 'iron man' cereals, it's on the back of the packets of muesli bars, and it's basically a weak approach to substantial physical change.

Although walking three times a week for 20 minutes is better than not walking at all, it's really only a warm-up, and not very good for *fat burning* and *muscle toning*, which is really why you're doing it!

The best length of time to walk is an hour, and the best number of days to walk a week is four to six. Anything under that is okay, *but your results will be in proportion with the amount of time and effort you put in.*

WHAT ABOUT FOOD AND DRINKS?

It's so important that you remember to take at least 500 mL of water with you when you are doing any form of physical exercise, including and *especially* walking. You may not think you will need it when you first step out, but you'll certainly be glad you brought it along at the end of a 5 km pacy walk!

The main thing to remember in combining your food with your exercise is *don't eat before you exercise.* The only people I know who eat before they exercise are certain sports men and women who require a carbohydrate boost.

Most of us, however, don't need a carbohydrate boost! Our biggest problem, besides eating too much fat, is an overload of carbohydrates.

The best thing to do is have plenty of water, day and night and especially when you're exercising, and make sure that you eat your breakfast as soon as you come home from your walk. This will also help to keep your metabolic rate at a speedy pace throughout the day.

Stay away from sports drinks unless you are being coached to drink them for sporting purposes. They are usually loaded with sugar.

For you, good old-fashioned water should suffice.

WHAT DO I WEAR?

Something you may notice when you begin walking, especially after the first few days, is that you will need some good walking shoes. Your shins and ankles will soon let you know by aching day and night until you do something about it.

What you need to look for in a suitable walking shoe is a good heel cushion, a flexible forefoot, plenty of room in the 'toe box' so that the shoes can spread during push-off, supporting heel construction for stability, and a low heel. Most good sports stores today have trained consultants on hand who are skilled at knowing which shoes will be best for the type of training you will be doing, coupled with the type of feet you have.

Make sure that you're dressed comfortably and coolly when you're exercising. Simple shorts or track pants with a t-shirt, and don't forget good supportive underwear – it's a must! It's also an idea to wear a hat, sunscreen and sunglasses if you decide to walk after around 7.30 am in summer and 8.30 am in winter.

The issue of hand weights has been debated by medical and exercise professionals for years. If you have high blood pressure, it's best that you walk without them. If, however, you are healthy, you can walk with them. Make sure you *use* your arm and shoulder muscles. Don't leave the weights dangling from your fingertips, and make sure you don't grip them too tightly.

WHY DO I STILL FEEL LIKE RUNNING?

Who knows! Except, many people do! I can understand if you still feel like running, even though I have told you to start walking, especially if you have always run and you are fairly active. But, I do need to stress that you consider *why* it is that you are running. If you want to run or jog for fitness – heart and lung fitness – go for it! If it's to get into shape, then *slow down!*

Unless you are already fit, all you will be doing by running or jogging is working at a rate which does not allow the body to absorb oxygen properly, so it uses other energies, because *fat needs oxygen to burn!*

If you want to burn fat, walk until you become fitter, then if you really like jogging or running, then slowly, slowly, slowly pick up the pace until you are not breathless. It's more important to not be breathless than it is for you to run a single kilometre!

Take my local park, for example. It's just over one kilometre per lap. If I were to walk for one hour, having completed six laps and without becoming breathless, I am much better off than running the six laps in 20 minutes, and collapsing in a heap at the end.

It really is re-education. You may need to re-train your mind, and try it out for yourself. *Go for it!*

Chapter 20

Muscle Toning and Strengthening

I can remember nearly knocking myself out session after session, trying to cram in up to ten aerobics classes a week, which was supposed to help me achieve all over muscle tone. Then I discovered resistance training, and everything changed from then on.

Using weights, or resistance training, offers tremendous body shaping benefits. Resistance training is any exercise that involves the muscles of the body attempting to move some type of opposing force. As a muscle is used, it is strengthened and toned. The more it's used, the more strengthened and toned it will be.

As you lift a window that may be a little stiff, you can feel the resistance in your forearms, biceps and the front of your shoulders. Just as the window force is downwards, and you are lifting upwards, there you have a form of resistance exercise.

It's important to remember when you are doing resistance training that you actually feel resistance in your muscles. If you don't feel that they are being 'worked', then they probably are not being 'worked'. On the other hand, it's important for you to get to know your body, and to get a feel for what muscle resistance is, and the uncomfortable feeling of using your muscles, versus pain in the joints, tendons and ligaments. It's good to 'feel' what your muscles are doing. It should feel 'hard', but not feel overly 'painful'. If any exercise feels too painful, you should stop immediately, and seek professional advice from a registered fitness leader.

We all want to feel great and look great, and be free to live the life we were created to live. In many studies carried out by various health and sporting bodies, it has been found that *muscle training keeps you young*. Now that's something we *ALL* want to know about! This relates to an increase in fitness, a decline in stress levels, an increase in muscular tone strength, a stability of bone density and good joint flexibility. All things we would certainly notice if we were without them!

The truth is, you do not need to do a lot of different exercises, only a few very basic ones, done correctly, to take you a long way towards your body toning goals.

Again, I want to encourage you to weigh up the initial 'discomfort' of exercise against years of being unhappy with yourself. You can plod away for years and years, watching aerobics videos and taking part as much as you can, and you won't see a fraction of the improvement that you will once you begin walking and using resistance training to tone your muscles.

Once you decide to get serious about what you really want, you are going to see for yourself how easy it all is – really!

> Weights or resistance training is the quickest proven method to change your body shape with the minimum amount of effort.

If you already consider yourself a 'fitness fanatic', then you will be aware of the incredible benefits of training with weights. If however, you are the exact opposite, then I'm here to help you become aware of the benefits!

Aerobic exercise, such as walking, is great for improving cardiovascular fitness (your heart), and improving muscular endurance in your legs, but contributes only a small amount to toning the rest of your body, and improving your overall flexibility, muscular endurance and strength, especially in your upper body.

Weight training is an activity that can be done in a short period, yet it makes dramatic changes to your body shape – and how you feel. Having toned muscles not only feels great, it also increases your energy level and improves your productivity at work and in many other everyday activities.

Training with weights helps to maintain muscle strength, muscular endurance, nerve-muscle (neuromuscular) co-ordination, and bone density, which helps to prevent osteoporosis, not to mention a whole range of other nasty medical conditions.

Research shows us that weight training makes a significant contribution to quality of life, whatever one's age or gender. And remember, it is a *fat burning* exercise!

One of the most difficult thought processes I had to overcome at first was that if I did any exercise with weights, that would mean that I would grow massive muscles, and end up looking like the *Incredible Hulkess*! However, this was not so! I discovered that to grow huge muscles took huge effort, huge amounts of body-building foods, and huge amounts of anabolic *you-know-whats*. So relax and know that your muscles are only going to become as big and toned as they can naturally, which can be very attractive.

If you know all your hard work is going to hit the mark, you'll invest much more time and energy into doing it. One of the greatest hurdles I had to overcome was moving from training in the aerobics room to training in the weights room – with all the big and sweaty 'grunters'. Many years ago, training with weights was not really heard of for any other purpose than body-building, weight lifting or for other sports which required great power and strength. The weights room was hardly the place to find a novice who simply wanted to get into better shape!

How times have changed! We now recognise that weight training was the best way all along.

> Weight training is for *everybody*,
> not just a select few.

I discovered that I was able to broaden my shoulder width by doing certain shoulder exercises and was able to tone up the back of my legs and buttocks by doing various hamstring and glute (bottom) exercises.

You may already be aware of all the wonderful benefits of resistance training. If not, I want to encourage you not to feel intimidated by something new, and something which has before now been associated with unwarranted fears about growing BIG hairy muscles! If only you knew how hard it is for body-builders to grow these things. It really does take a great deal of time, energy and food to end up like one!

It wasn't until I started resistance training that I finally had the true results I wanted. Aerobics was keeping me fit on the inside, which is important, but the muscle tone just wasn't there. When I started to use weights, the shape of my legs changed, and I became much stronger and fitter in the process.

Instead of having string-bean legs, I actually developed some shape in the front of my thighs. And, even more amazingly, my inner thighs and back of my thighs slimmed right down and toned right up, in proportion with the rest of my legs.

Until I properly understood the body shaping benefits of resistance training, I limited myself to simply dreaming about any kind of substantial improvement.

One great result of resistance training is that it will help give you the ability to go shopping and carry massive loads of shopping bags without any difficulty! Your back will be strengthened and your shoulders and arms will be much stronger than ever before. And you won't bulge with massive muscles, but instead you will have nicely toned muscle shape.

Another great result of resistance training is that your stamina is increased. You will no longer be lethargic and puffed out when walking, or climbing stairs, but instead feel as though a huge weight has been lifed from your shoulders.

> If the ladder is not leaning against the right wall, every step you take just gets you to the wrong place faster!
>
> Stephen R. Covey

It's time to lean against the right wall, to walk up the right path, to do those things that will take us to the *right* place faster! If you are doing countless amounts of exercise already and not getting the results you need, it's time to stop and re-evaluate how you are spending your time.

First of all you need to ensure that you are feeding your muscles properly with a good diet, high in protein. You also need to ensure that the exercise you are doing is helping your body to become the fat burning, muscle toning, energy building machine that it was created to be.

HOW LONG AND HOW HARD SHOULD I TRAIN?

Although there is an obvious advantage with walking as you don't require equipment, there is an obvious advantage in your *body toning progress* with weight training.

Unlike other exercise activities that rely on developing specific muscles, for example, legs for walking or cycling, weight training programs can be designed to develop your legs as well as many other muscle groups.

You would be surprised with the fitness levels of many body-builders who don't run marathons, but instead walk, cycle or use a stepper machine, and train with weights. Those who train consistently are extremely fit! Training with weights can be a 'cardio', fat burning experience when done properly. Providing the training session is approximately 45 minutes in length, and is carried out at a heart rate of approximately 110–120 beats per minute, then your fitness level will rise, and fat burning will take place.

By increasing muscle tone (and they don't have to be huge), you are making your body into a well-tuned machine, able to burn fat. If your body has well-toned muscle tissue, and you eat a well-balanced diet, with plenty of protein and water, it will always use up its store of fat first!

This means that once you have improved your muscle tone through weight training, and you have been eating right, you are able to be less strict with your food intake. It's a fact that the difference between people who are overweight and those who are not is not necessarily the food intake as much as the lack of physical activity.

If you can't exercise for whatever reason, you are still able to have a great body shape through eating right, but if you want a great body shape which is toned and which frees you up from being so strict with your food intake, then walk and train with weights. It's that simple!

What makes weight training exciting is the rapid rate at which you can see and feel changes in your body! As soon as you begin exercising, your muscles feel firmer, and the body toning process begins. Regular training will convince you that you have the ability to tone your body better than you may ever have expected!

Although you can't grow new muscles, you can change the tone and shape of your muscles, whatever your body type, and so bridge the gap between the physique you want and the one you look at every day in the mirror! Toned muscles look and feel great; they don't droop at the back of your arms, or sag at your waist. If you follow the instructions properly in this book, you will find this out for yourself!

HOW OFTEN SHOULD I TRAIN?

You really should exercise a muscle three to four times each week to achieve good muscle tone. Exercising more than that may speed your progress, but you must be careful not to overdo it. Sometimes, the greatest enthusiasts end up being the most injured! Once you've made up your mind to train with weights, it's important to take it one step at a time, and if you're a beginner, then start as a beginner. It's pointless knocking yourself out in the first week, and then being unable to train for the next three weeks because you're too sore and can't move!

The length of your training session will depend on what stage you're up to and which body parts you're training. Somewhere between 30 and 45 minutes is a good indication. You should be training *hard*. This doesn't mean that you should be trying to kill yourself, but you should be using *effort* in everything you do. Just as when you're walking it's important to walk with good posture and to concentrate on the muscles you're using, the same applies to weight training.

If you can concentrate on what you're doing, you will tone your muscles in a much shorter period of time. If you squeeze your legs while doing lunges, for example, your legs will be getting a double workout, in half the time, and the benefits are twice as impressive!

WHERE SHOULD I TRAIN?

The obvious and best place to train, if you can afford it, is your local gym. They have spent literally hundreds of thousands of dollars on equipment and maintenance of equipment, for you to benefit from. All you have to do is turn up, use it at your leisure, and leave, without giving it a second thought – except, of course, for the initial gym membership cost.

If you decide to set up a home gym, you may like to first consider the cost, then the inconvenience of having equipment taking up space in your home. There is the advantage of privacy if you'd like it, but exercising can become boring if you don't have any contact with anyone.

The best solution, if you can't afford gym membership, is to buy yourself a good pair of dumbbells and use them at home. Sometimes it's not even money – it's time and convenience, as I've spoken about previously. If you have kids at home, or if you work strange hours, you are much better off following a routine that doesn't mean you have to be somewhere else to do it.

Put up pictures of what the new you is going to look like, and empty out your kitchen cupboards and fridge. If you're going to train at home, at least make it easier on yourself!

WHAT ABOUT MY AGE AND STAGE?

I don't believe there should be any limits placed on anyone because of age and stage of development. Probably the youngest suggested age for weight training is around 16 years, to be safe, although there are a number of teenagers, especially guys, who start earlier than this. Teenagers should be careful with weight training to ensure that their bones have developed sufficiently to cope with the weights being used.

As far as the other end of the scale is concerned, it doesn't matter how *old* you are either. Many awesome body-builders are still at world-class competition level at 50 to 65 years of age! The earlier you start and the more consistent you are with weights, the longer you will look and feel great.

If you are a beginner, take heart – you won't be for long. Everybody has to start somewhere at some time, and if this is your time – great! Before too long you will be glad you decided to do something about your physique that would be long lasting in appearance, and fun in the process.

A lean, well-proportioned body *only* comes
from losing body fat and gaining muscle!

CAN I 'SPOT REDUCE'?

One vital point to remember is that you *cannot* 'spot reduce'. In other words, if you have a roll of fat on your tummy, doing 1000 sit-ups three times a day is not going to get rid of it. The result of this type of over-exercising will widen the stomach, not slim it!

YOU WILL NOT NECESSARILY BE BURNING FAT from the area you are training. The reason you are doing weight resistance training is to firm your muscles and increase your body's ability as a whole to burn fat from wherever it sees fit. And believe me, it's often not our choice of fat store that goes first, eg breasts or face. In fact, the general rule is, the bigger the fat store – eg bottom, hips and thighs – the more it is likely that the body will leave it until last. So it's vitally important to be patient, and persistent – especially now you know why. The best part of living this lifestyle is that you will notice body fat gone from places you never thought possible!

GOOD POSTURE

One of the most important factors when doing any kind of physical exercise is posture. If you have good posture, you are already off to a good start. If not, it's the first thing I want to work on with you.

If your posture is not good, it needs correcting. If you don't correct your posture, and you begin exercising, especially with weights, all you will be doing is adding to your problem.

If your shoulders are already rounded because of the way you have stood or sat for years and years, it's now time to straighten up! If you don't, you may injure your joints and tendons.

So, shoulders back, head up, joints slightly relaxed to soften the stress, and off you go! Keep it simple – keep it *possible* and *achievable*!

SAFETY TIPS

Weight training includes the use of dumbbells, barbells, and/or machinery. When you are doing an exercise with a bar or dumbbells, it's important that you check that the weight is not too heavy for you. It's also important that you don't have it too light, as you won't improve unless your muscles are used!

If possible, exercise in front of a mirror, so you can continually check your form and posture.

If you are doing any exercise which requires you to lift the weight above your head, it would be wise for you to use a training partner to assist you if necessary.

Always hold your stomach in tight while exercising. Not only does this provide good support for your lower back, but it will help tone your stomach muscles in the process!

During exercises where you are required to stand, always keep your knees just slightly bent to ensure the muscles surrounding your knees are providing the necessary support.

If you are a beginner, lift light weights until you can perform a particular exercise correctly. Remember, good form is always more important than heavy weights. If you have to hunch over, swing your back and break your arm to lift a mega-sized dumbbell, you are wasting your time.

When lifting heavy weights, always lift with your knees. Using the muscles in your hips and thighs, bend down to the weight and pick it up. Don't use your back – *ever!* This same rule applies when picking up anything heavy, be it groceries, children, *anything!*

It's important also to keep the weight close to your body. This will ensure controlled movement and beneficial muscle toning.

Remembering all the safety tips, you also need to know that to effectively train a muscle to become stronger and more toned, you need to stimulate your muscles by working them. This is called 'overload'. It means taking your muscles one step further on in strength and endurance each time you use them.

You need to proceed carefully with overloading your muscles, as sometimes over-keenness can bring about injury. Gradually combine overload with rest, and remember that it's the *overload* which stimulates the muscles to be stronger and more toned, and it's the *rest* which provides the room to do so.

EQUIPMENT

Although many weight training exercises include the use of training equipment – dumbbells, barbells, or machinery – there should also be enough props around your home to keep you very busy in the comfort of your own home. Furniture, a broomstick and even a couple of cans of baked beans, instead of dumbbells, will work!

I do recommend, however, that you buy yourself a pair of dumbbells, as these aren't very expensive and will be most useful. Don't get them too light, but don't go overboard with weight if you are a beginner. If you're just starting out, somewhere between two and five kilos for each dumbbell will be sufficient.

If you want to buy a bar without weights attached, these weigh around six kilos, which will give you good resistance. And, as you improve and become stronger, you can add weights to the ends of the bar.

An exercise mat is also a good idea for your floor exercises. If you don't have one, simply lay a towel down onto carpet. This is usually all the comfort you would get at the gym anyway!

There are many home gyms and machines available. The best thing to do is decide for yourself what you really need them for and also consider the cost and space they take up.

If you can, find a good gym and buy yourself a membership, which will give easy access to all the equipment you will need. Shop around as some offer good deals to new clients.

Always train in comfortable clothes and supportive shoes.

Remember your priorities!

> Train to look good, rather than worrying about looking good to train!

If you are training at the gym, especially, wear something that can get dirty and sweaty. Please don't spend hundreds of dollars to make a fashion statement here – but spend it afterwards instead by all means!

STRETCHING

It's really important to prepare your body for exercise. Just as you prepare for work in the morning by having a shower, getting dressed and eating your breakfast, you need to prepare your body for exercise by warming up and stretching. If you don't prepare your muscles for exercise correctly, you will be prone to injuries, and that's the bottom line. You will get much more out of a muscle the warmer it is. Once the blood is flowing to a particular muscle group, it is ready for exercise. You'll notice that professional dancers always warm up. You need to become a professional body toner. You always need to warm up. A good warm-up session can increase your metabolic rate, and hence start fat burning, before you even begin your training routine.

It's also important to cool down and stretch after exercising. I can remember numerous times when I've worked out with weights, and gone straight home in a rush *before* cooling down and stretching properly, only to find I couldn't move the next day, or three! *Ouch!*

UPPER BODY

Broad shoulders, a taut chest, firm arms,
toned stomach and strong back.
You can do it!

Most people aren't really aware of all the different muscles in their body. Biceps (front of upper arms), triceps (back of upper arm) and pectorals (chest) are probably the most well-known in the upper body. Together with trapezius (top of shoulders), deltoids (back of shoulders) and latissimus of the back (sides of the back), they make up the muscles associated with a classic physique.

The upper body has been shown through studies to suffer the most neglect. Without a strong upper half, it is impossible to even do one push-up! Women are renowned for being weak in the upper body, with flabbiness being a common problem in the back of their arms.

But the good news is that because the upper body is usually neglected, it is often quick to respond to training, and the results can be very impressive.

Broadened shoulders give an appearance that your hips are slimmer. Firmly toned arms look great in sleeveless shirts and a strong back always looks great in a swimsuit or backless dress.

Because everyone is different with regards to strength and personal goals, it's important to determine what is going to be right for you. Make sure you don't become carried away with improving one body part, as this will lead to imbalance and can cause injury and joint problems.

It's really important, as I mentioned previously with regards to posture, that your body position is maintained during exercise. If you rock back and forth from the hips while doing bicep curls, for example, not only will this be easier for you, and therefore less effective, but you may even suffer back strain in the process. It's not worth cheating to make things easier, because in the long run, you won't achieve your goals, and you may land yourself a nasty injury.

Having a toned upper half means that your head is held erect, your chest is strong and uplifted and your shoulders are relaxed and even. Opening heavy doors and carrying a dozen grocery bags should no longer pose a problem!

LOWER BODY

Your largest muscles, and potentially the most developed ones, are most likely to be found in your lower body. This is because your hips and legs have to support and move the rest of your body. For the average sized adult, this means carrying more than 45 kilograms.

Your lower body muscles can be slower to show the effects of training, because of lack of use. In turn this lack of use can result in a more noticeable, saggy appearance.

Also, it can be harder to train and improve the lower body muscles because they aren't as easy to 'overload' as the upper body muscles.

However, *all* can be improved!

Muscle-toning exercises alone will not slim your thighs, but they will improve your appearance by firming and toning muscle tissue as you lose weight. The only way to lose fat and get rid of lumps and bumps is to watch what you're eating and increase your energy output.

A strong and well-toned lower half will make you feel great and look great. You will find that the more exercise you do with your lower body, the easier it will get. Remember though, careful overload is what brings about great results, so don't get lazy or too comfortable doing any exercises – especially with your legs and bottom!

If you've ever looked at some legs and wondered how it is that they have such great shape, it's either because of genetics, and good use of them (a mesomorph who uses what they have), or it's sheer hard work using resistance training (weights).

The great news is, because of resistance training, it doesn't matter what your current physical shape is, you can change it. Using weights is really a body sculpting process, where your muscle begins to strengthen and take great shape, and your body fat reduces through walking and eating 'fat free'!

If you do 1000 sit-ups a day and don't change your eating habits, you won't change your stomach. But, if you eat 'fat free' and do a sensible, well-balanced amount of exercise, your stomach will look outstanding, and in hardly any time at all!

Remember that balance is important. Not only balancing weights – *so you don't drop them on your toes* – but balancing the whole diet and exercise thing.

This is the bottom line – if you want to look great, feel great, work, sleep and play well, then you have to …

... eat well and exercise consistently forever!

Chapter 21

Getting It Right

Most people know about lunges, leg raises and squats – the stuff that fitness videos get you doing in your living room. Exercise is a mind-blowing, complex issue, with numerous different types, styles and fads, and it's changing all the time.

This is not a bad thing, as everybody has different responses to different types of exercise. If I give you some vital points on resistance exercising, you can apply them to any routine or programme you may have been given in the past.

Even the old exercise video in your loungeroom can work wonders when you know what you're doing and *why*. No matter how average the programme you choose, or how little you know about training, if you follow *exactly* the following rules, *it will work*.

1   Find out exactly which area you are working when you exercise. If you are not completely sure, ask someone

who knows. It's the most crucial part of training. When you know it, write it down.

2   When doing the exercise, concentrate completely on the area you are supposed to be working. Don't think about what's for dinner, or where you have to be next, or what the kids are doing.

We all know someone who has been training for years and still looks little different from when they started. Almost always this is due to lack of focus. They go through the motions without any thought to what is and isn't working. Don't waste your time – CONCEN-TRATE!

3   If you cannot feel an exercise where you are sup-posed to, yet you are feeling it in an area you're not trying to work, simply adjust your position until you feel it where you should. Don't be afraid to shuffle your body into the correct position. Just because someone tells you that you are supposed to do it like this or that, it's really irrelevant if you can't feel it, or if it's working a totally different area. Everyone is built differently, so make it work for you.

4   Effort is vital. Do not worry about how many times you are supposed to repeat an exercise. The rule is easy – keep going until you can't go any more (at the same time, feeling it where you are supposed to), then *stop* and rest until you feel ready. Then do it again. Repeat this three or four times, or even up to five times, depending on how you feel.

Remember to monitor yourself carefully, so you don't overdo it in the beginning. Obviously, if you are unfit, you won't be able to do much, and if you are fit, you'll be able to do a lot more. By following this, you will improve the muscle every time you train it, instead of stopping just about when the exercise starts to work for you.

5   Each time you do each exercise, do just a little more, building up slowly. It's a lot of fun and very inspirational to see how quickly you can improve.

6   Don't rush an exercise. Do them all slowly and deliberately, being aware of what is working through the up (bending or flexing) and the down (stretching or extending) of the movement.

> Remember, when combining aerobic activity (walking, cycling, etc) with weight training, to do them in the *correct order*.

Because your body burns up energy, or glycogen, when it first starts training, it's important that you weight train first. Then, when you start your aerobic training, you will be instantly burning fat. If you do it the other way around, not only will you be lacking energy to weight train, but you have wasted the first half of your aerobic training burning energy, and not fat! Simple but effective.

In summary, by applying the above principles, you will guarantee results. It is essential, however, that you apply *all* of them *all* the time. They are quite literally the key that makes the difference between those who shape up and those who don't.

The following chart has been designed as a simple guide with which you can assess your own programme.

Do whatever you can fit into your schedule, and try to make improvements over time, as you become more comfortable with the exercise.

BODY SHAPING EXERCISE CHART

Type of exercise	No. of days per week	Duration per day
Fat burning		
Walking or cycling	3–5 days	30–60 minutes
Muscle tone		
Weights	3–5 days	30–60 minutes

Don't eat before exercising, and try to eat 30 minutes after you've finished.

Effort in = Great results!

Chapter 22

Final FAQ

WHEN WILL I SEE RESULTS?

You will start to actually feel different from two to three weeks, and begin to look different from three to five weeks. The most dramatic results will come in six to eight weeks. This is when it will show not only in your physique, but also in your face. People will ask you, '*What's different?*', just as they would if you've had a new haircut. You won't look drawn and tired. You will have a greater energy level, and because you'll be sleeping better (a positive side effect of the *Fat Free Forever!* lifestyle), you will literally be bright eyed and bushy tailed! The results will keep on keeping on, for as long as you want. You may decide to be really careful for up to twelve weeks, then relax a little for the next week or two, then go back on for another four to six weeks. It can be in as many stages as you want.

WHEN CAN I WEIGH MYSELF?

You would by now have noticed that I haven't asked you to weigh yourself, and it's for a very good reason. Muscle weighs three times more than fat, so you aren't going to get a true picture of how well you're really doing with your new *Fat Free Forever!* lifestyle if you're constantly checking for dropped kilos, instead of checking for dropped inches. By all means, weigh yourself, but please don't become obsessed with it.

WHAT ABOUT AEROBICS?

Let's take a brief look at the aerobic activity which goes on at your local gym or health club, and how beneficial it actually is (or isn't) with regards to fat loss and muscle tone. One of the hardest things to do, especially if you have kids, is to wake up at some unearthly hour, switch on the TV (feeling absolutely gorgeous – not!), and suddenly find yourself watching half a dozen unbelievable bodies taking part in a perfectly choreographed aerobics routine. It's 6 am, and they're smiling – but you're not! Take heart. The fact of the matter is that these guys don't just do aerobics classes to look like that. They walk or do other cardio activities, each day, and they train in the gym – yes, with weights! If you enjoy doing aerobics classes, whether high or low, step, slide, box, funk, circuit, bums, tums or all of the above, by all means continue, but do consider why you are doing them!

WHAT ABOUT SPORT?

Sport is great, and I encourage young people to take part in some sport each week, especially in their developing years. People involved in sport are usually outgoing, positive and energetic – the type of people that others like being around. However, it's important for us not to confuse these benefits with body shaping benefits. Body shapers too are usually outgoing and energetic, and their physical shape is one of the major benefits of playing their type of sport!

Although I encourage people to take part in sport, especially in my own family (my boys love soccer, swimming and running), it's another ball park when it comes to fat loss and muscle toning. If you are into sport (playing it, and not just watching it), and it's for fun or fitness – great! But, if it's only for fat loss and muscle toning – forget it! You can still do sport because you enjoy it, but remember what I said about specificity of exercise and how important it is to be specific with what exercise you do.

HOW DO I MAINTAIN MY NEW BODY SHAPE?

By maintaining the *Fat Free Forever!* lifestyle. It's important to remember that you can do as much or as little of what has been suggested as you choose – and you can do it for as long or as short as you wish. If you want to maintain your new improved body shape, all you have to remember is the principles that gave you the new shape. When you've achieved your goal, your metabolism will be naturally faster, and you can probably even afford to occasionally have a couple of Junk Days per week. Because of the foundation you have laid in stripping body fat instead of muscle tissue and water, you will find that weight doesn't pour back on if you go off the rails for a while. Just remember what you put into achieving your new body shape, and that should be reason enough to keep a close check on what you eat in future.

HOW CAN SOME PEOPLE BE THIN, YET STILL FAT?

Ever noticed how even the skinniest girl in short shorts can still have dimply, flabby legs? This is because the muscle tissue has been starved by poor nutrition and severe lack of exercise. That's why even some 'bigger' girls look great, because they are a healthy size, with low body fat. It's the naked you which really counts and shows how healthy you are. I'd much rather be a healthy size 10–12 with no cellulite, thank you!

HOW LONG WILL IT TAKE FOR MY METABOLISM TO CHANGE?

The average time it takes for a sluggish metabolism to speed up is six to eight weeks. Of course, your genetics, fitness levels, and how careful you are at living the *Fat*

Free Forever! lifestyle will determine how long it takes you personally. The main thing to remember is that if you live the lifestyle, your metabolism will change. So, be encouraged, have patience, and just keep going until it does!

100 Fat Free Recipes

You know by now that the *Fat Free Forever!* lifestyle says, 'If you can see the fat, it's too much'. As there are enough natural fats in foods, I have designed recipes and cooking methods around utilising this minimal amount of unseen fat.

What is unique about the Fat Free Recipes is the coding system, which has been designed to make life easier for you. You can quickly turn to any recipe and not have to work out if it's protein, carbs, or the time of day it should be eaten. When you start using the recipes, you will soon become aware of these without even looking.

FAT FREE RECIPES CODING SYSTEM

Each recipe has three faces at the top of the page.

☺ **eat it and enjoy**

😐 **eat it if you must**
(something else would be better)

☹ **don't eat it now!**

B, **D** and **L** are written beneath the faces, and they indicate when you can eat each recipe.

B Breakfast

L Lunch

D Dinner

LIST OF FAT FREE RECIPES

Pasta

Rice

Desserts

Snacks

Party Appetisers

Dianne's Favourites

Farmhouse Muesli

Big Breakfast

Penne with Tomatoes and Basil

Unfried Chicken Strips

Springtime Stir Fry

B   L   D

Farmhouse Muesli

Large Starchy Carbohydrate/
Small Fibrous Carbohydrate
20 minutes to make
Serves 2 adults

Ingredients

½ cup dried prunes
½ cup dried apricots
2 cups hot water
2 cups quick cooking oats
4 tablespoons 97–98% fat free muesli
2–3 cups skim milk

Method

1 Heat prunes and apricots in hot water in the microwave for 10–20 minutes, depending on what type of microwave you have, and let sit until plump.

2 Into a medium non-stick saucepan, place oats, muesli and milk. Stir thoroughly. If possible, allow to soak cold for 10–15 minutes.

3 Cook on a low to medium heat for approximately 10 minutes, ensuring a creamy texture. Add a little more milk if necessary. Make sure the mixture isn't gluggy.

4 Serve piping hot with warm prunes, apricots and honey, and a dollop of natural fat free yoghurt, if desired.

Big Breakfast

B   L   D

Large Protein/Medium Carbohydrate (optional)
20 minutes to make
Serves 2 adults

Ingredients

4 slices 98% fat free smoked ham
½ cup fat free chicken stock
2 large ripe tomatoes
handful fresh button mushrooms
your choice of eggs

Method

1 Begin cooking ham in half the chicken stock in a small non-stick frypan. Cover with a lid after one side has browned. Add a little extra water if necessary.
2 In a separate frypan, cook the tomatoes in chunks, along with the mushrooms and the remaining chicken stock.
3 Cook your choice of eggs as per the recipes in the Eggs section (pp. 189–193).
4 Serve immediately with toast (no butter) and some Chipped Potato Grits (p. 268). (No toast and no potatoes if you are eating this meal for dinner.)

B L D

Penne with Tomatoes and Basil

Large Carbohydrate/Small Protein
20 minutes to make
Serves at least 4 adults

Ingredients

3 cups water
1 small packet penne pasta
2 tins whole peeled tomatoes (without oil and, if
    possible, without sugar)
2 teaspoons fresh or 1 teaspoon dried basil
1/2 teaspoon salt
1/2 teaspoon pepper
1/4 cup chopped spring onions
1 teaspoon crushed garlic
1/4 cup red wine

Method

1 In a large saucepan, boil the water, and add the penne. Add more water if necessary. Cook only until soft. It takes approximately 15 minutes.
2 Place the rest of the ingredients in a medium-sized non-stick saucepan. Stir well and simmer on low–medium heat for 30 minutes, or until liquid is fairly reduced.
3 Drain and wash the pasta well and place it into a large container for serving.
4 Pour the sauce over the pasta and mix well.
5 Serve with a fresh side salad (no parmesan cheese!).

Unfried Chicken Strips

B L D

Large Protein
15 minutes to make
Serves 4 adults

Ingredients

3 double chicken breast fillets (skinless and boneless)
1½ cups self-raising flour
¾ cup Cajun spices
4 eggs (1 yolk only)
⅓ cup teriyaki sauce
pepper and salt to taste

Method

1 Wash chicken and remove any traces of fat. Cut each half breast into 4 strips.
2 Empty the flour, spices, salt and pepper onto greaseproof paper and mix thoroughly.
3 In a separate bowl, whisk the eggs with the teriyaki sauce.
4 Heat a large non-stick frypan on high until the pan is really hot.
5 Roll each chicken strip in the flour mixture, then dip in the egg mixture, then into the flour mixture again.
6 Place strips straight into the hot pan. Cover with a lid.
7 After 5–7 minutes, turn the strips over (they should look greyish). Replace the lid and cook a further 3–4 minutes.
8 Remove lid and splash a little water over chicken so it starts to look golden. Replace lid. It's important that there are no puddles of water in the pan. Turn and splash until the golden colour comes through most of each strip.
9 Cook for a further 2 minutes. Remove.

This frying/steaming combination creates a great taste while keeping the chicken moist and succulent.

Springtime Stir Fry

B L D

Medium Carbohydrate
20 minutes to make
Serves 4 adults

Ingredients

2 cups fresh green beans
1 cup fresh snow peas
1 cup shredded butternut pumpkin
1 cup shredded cabbage
½ cup bean sprouts
½ cup fat free vegetable stock
1 teaspoon Cajun spices
salt and pepper to taste
½ cup white wine

Method

1 Preheat a large non-stick frypan while preparing vegetables.
2 Combine all the ingredients, place in frypan
   and place a lid on top.
3 After 10 minutes or so, stir and replace the lid.
4 Remove when vegies are just cooked.
5 Serve hot on its own, or with some grilled chicken strips.

Protein Shakes

Strawberry Smoothie

Passionfruit Malt Shake

Crushed Fruit Splice

Iced Coffee Shake

Double Chocolate Shake

B   L   D

Strawberry Smoothie

Large Protein
2 minutes to make
Serves 1 adult

Ingredients

2 cups skim milk
3 heaped dessertspoons whey protein isolate or whey
      protein concentrate powder
handful fresh strawberries
200 grams fat free strawberry flavoured yoghurt

Method

1   Using a container which will hold up to 3 cups of liquid, pour in the milk. *(Make <u>sure</u> the milk is added first!)*
2   Add the other ingredients.
3   Blend well.
4   Drink straightaway while chilled, or take with you in a flask to drink throughout the day.

Passionfruit Malt Shake

B L D

Large Protein
2 minutes to make
Serves 1 adult

Ingredients

2 cups skim milk
3 heaped dessertspoons whey protein isolate or whey
    protein concentrate powder
200 grams fat free passionfruit yoghurt
pulp of 1 small, fresh passionfruit (if in season)
1 heaped teaspoon malt
3 dessertspoons no-fat, low-sugar natural yoghurt

Method

1 Using a container which will hold up to 3 cups of liquid,
   pour in the milk. *(Make <u>sure</u> the milk is added first!)*
2 Add the other ingredients.
3 Blend well.
4 Drink straightaway while chilled, or take with you in a
   flask to drink throughout the day.

B L D

Crushed Fruit Splice

Large Protein
Takes 2 minutes to make
Serves 1 adult

Ingredients

2 cups skim milk
2 cups 100% apple juice (no added sugar)
3 dessertspoons low-fat, no-sugar natural yoghurt
3 heaped dessertspoons whey protein isolate or whey
   protein concentrate powder
½ cup fresh fruit, roughly chopped (no banana)
½ cup ice

Method

1 Using a hand-held or bench-top blender, crush ice and fruit.
2 Add the other ingredients.
3 Blend well.
4 Serve with a garnish of fresh strawberries.

B   L   D

Iced Coffee Shake

Large Protein
2 minutes to make
Serves 1 adult

Ingredients

2 cups skim milk
3 heaped dessertspoons whey protein isolate or whey
    protein concentrate powder
½ cup espresso coffee (poured)
1 teaspoon artificial sweetener (to taste)

Method

1 Using a container that can hold 3 cups, pour in the milk.
   (Make <u>sure</u> the milk is added first!)
2 Add the other ingredients.
3 Blend well.
4 Drink while chilled, or take with you in a flask to drink
   throughout the day.

Double Chocolate Shake

B L D

Large Protein
2 minutes to make
Serves 1 adult

Ingredients

- 2 cups skim milk
- 3 heaped dessertspoons whey protein isolate or whey protein concentrate powder
- 3 dessertspoons fat free chocolate sauce

Method

1 Using a container which will hold up to 3 cups of liquid, pour in the milk. *(Make <u>sure</u> the milk is added first!)*
2 Add the other ingredients.
3 Blend well.
4 Drink while chilled, or take with you in a flask to drink throughout the day.

Eggs

Gourmet Scrambled Eggs

French Toast

Fresh Vegetable Omelette

Toad in the Hole

Curried Egg and Lettuce Sandwiches

Gourmet Scrambled Eggs

B   L   D

Large Protein/Small Carbohydrate (optional)
10 minutes to make
Serves 2 adults

Ingredients

10 large eggs
2 teaspoons freshly chopped parsley
½ cup skim milk
salt and pepper to taste
4 pieces thickly sliced bread for toasting
   (only if it's breakfast or lunch)
fat free seasoning sauce to taste

Method

1   Remove 6 out of 10 yolks.
2   Heat a medium non-stick frypan and add all the ingredients. Stir occasionally.
3   When the eggs are nearly cooked, remove from the heat, stirring from the base of the pan.
4   Serve immediately on hot, unbuttered toast (no toast if eating for dinner) with a drizzle of seasoning sauce.

Note If you accidentally cook the eggs right through, add another whole egg and mix quickly through the scrambled eggs. This should make them nice and creamy again.

B   L   D

French Toast

Medium Protein/Medium Carbohydrate
5 minutes to make
Serves 2 adults

Ingredients

1 tank loaf white bread
4 large eggs
2 tablespoons skim milk
salt and pepper to taste
1 tomato *or* maple syrup

Method

1 Slice 4 pieces of bread approximately 2 cm thick.
2 In a medium bowl, whisk the eggs, milk, salt and pepper.
3 Briefly soak each slice of bread in the egg mixture.
4 Heat a large non-stick frypan. Place the soaked bread in pan.
5 When browned, turn the bread over.
6 When both sides are browned, serve with grilled tomatoes or, if you've been good, a small dash of maple syrup!

Fresh Vegetable Omelette

B   L   D

Large Protein
10 minutes to make
Serves 1 adult

Ingredients

4 large eggs (2 yolks only)
2 teaspoons parsley, freshly chopped
1 teaspoon fat free vegetable stock powder
1 small tomato, chopped
½ small onion, chopped
½ cup spring onions, chopped
1 cup crunchy vegetables, freshly chopped
salt and pepper to taste

Method

1 Beat eggs well in a medium mixing bowl.
2 Add remaining ingredients.
3 Heat a medium non-stick frypan and add the mixture.
4 When the base is cooked and coming away from the sides of the pan, remove the omelette from the stove and place under a preheated griller until the mixture is well cooked and lightly browned on top.
5 Remove the omelette carefully by folding one half on top of the other, then sliding it onto a warmed plate.
6 Serve with a crunchy garden salad.

B   L   D

Toad in the Hole

Medium Protein/Medium Carbohydrate
15 minutes to make
Serves 1 adult

Ingredients

3 large eggs
1 teaspoon parsley, freshly chopped
salt and pepper to taste
2 thick slices white or wholemeal bread
1 ripe tomato
fat free seasoning sauce to taste

Method

1 In a small mixing bowl, beat 1 egg and add the parsley, salt and pepper.
2 Cut out a small square in the middle of each slice of bread – the size of an egg yolk.
3 Dip the bread in the egg mixture.
4 Heat a large non-stick frypan and add the bread.
5 Crack 1 egg into the middle of each slice of bread.
6 Place a lid on the pan, and as soon as the bottom of the bread is browned, carefully turn over.
7 Depending on whether you like your eggs runny or hard, remove accordingly.
8 Serve hot with grilled tomatoes, fresh parsley and a sprinkle of seasoning sauce.

Curried Egg and Lettuce Sandwiches   B   L   D

Medium Protein/Medium Carbohydrate
15 minutes to make
Serves 2 adults

Ingredients

3 large eggs
8 thick slices white *or* wholemeal bread
1 teaspoon curry powder
2 teaspoons tomato sauce
1 tablespoon skim milk (plus a little extra if required)
1 tablespoon fat free salad dressing
1 teaspoon parsley, freshly chopped
salt and pepper to taste
lettuce

Method

1   In a small saucepan, hard boil the eggs.
2   Remove when cooked (approximately 10 minutes), and peel shell under cold water.
3   In a small mixing bowl, place the eggs and other ingredients.
4   Mix thoroughly until nice and creamy, adding extra milk if necessary.
5   Chop the lettuce finely.
6   Spoon egg mixture onto bread and sprinkle lettuce on top.
7   Cut sandwiches into fingers and serve with a garnish of fresh parsley.

Fish

Creamy Tuna Mornay

Grilled Fish with Lemon and Herbs

Baked Fish with Tomato Seasoning

Red Salmon Salad

Tuna Chowder

Creamy Tuna Mornay

B L D

Large Protein/Medium Carbohydrate (optional)
15 minutes to make
Serves 4 adults

Ingredients

4 eggs
1½ cups white rice
4 cups water
1 low fat cheese sauce packet mix
1 low fat stroganoff sauce packet mix
2 cups skim milk
425 gram tin of tuna in brine or springwater
1 small onion, chopped finely
salt and pepper to taste
1 lemon

Method

1 Hard boil eggs in small saucepan.
2 Boil rice in medium saucepan in water. Be careful not to overcook. Add more water if necessary.
3 Place cheese and stroganoff sauce mixes in a medium non-stick saucepan with the milk. Whisk well and keep stirring over a medium heat.
4 Drain the tuna. When the sauce is thickened, add tuna to the sauce. Add extra milk or brine if necessary to ensure mixture doesn't become gluggy. Add the onion.
5 Chop eggs into chunks and add to the tuna and sauce, along with salt and pepper.
6 Serve hot on a bed of rice with a slice of lemon. (No rice if you eat this dish in the evening.)

Grilled Fish with Lemon and Herbs   B L D

Large Protein/Small Fibrous Carbohydrate
10 minutes to make
Serves 4 adults

Ingredients

- 4 large fillets of fresh, fleshy white fish (trevally, snapper, roughie)
- 4 squares of foil big enough to envelop fish fillets
- 2 teaspoons mixed herbs
- 2 lemons
- pepper and salt to taste

Method

1. Wash fish and place individually in the centre of each piece of foil.
2. Add herbs, a good squeeze of lemon, and a generous amount of salt and pepper.
3. Make a little package of the foil so no lemon juice escapes.
4. Close the packages like a pastie with the seam on top.
5. Place on a tray and, under a medium–high heat, grill for approximately 7 minutes.
6. Open packages and return to grill for another few minutes until the fish starts to brown.
7. Serve with a wedge of lemon and fresh garden salad.

B   L   D

Baked Fish with Tomato Seasoning

Medium Protein

45 minutes to make
Serves 4 adults

Ingredients

1 deep-sea bream (gutted and scaled)
1 large tomato
1 large onion
1 lemon
2 spring onion stalks
1 dessertspoon salt

Method

1 Wash the fish thoroughly and place on a large sheet of foil (big enough to fold over).
2 Slice the tomato, onion and lemon in circles.
3 Chop the spring onions (not too finely).
4 Spread the ingredients on top of the fish. Add salt.
5 Wrap foil over the fish and bake for approximately 30 minutes at 180°C (350°F).
6 Serve with your favourite non-starch salad and fat free dressing.

B L D

Red Salmon Salad

Large Protein/Medium Carbohydrate (optional)
10 minutes to make
Serves 4 adults

Ingredients

425 gram tin of red salmon, drained well
1 small onion, finely chopped
1 tablespoon parsley, freshly chopped
2 medium carrots, roughly chopped
2 large celery stalks, roughly chopped
1/2 a red or green (or both) capsicum, roughly chopped
1/4 cup lemon juice
fat free French or Italian salad dressing
salt and pepper to taste

Method

1 Place all ingredients in a large mixing bowl and mix thoroughly.
2 Serve either hot or cold over white rice or with a dry-baked jacket potato (only if you're eating this for lunch). You can serve it with a green salad for early dinner.

B L D

Tuna Chowder

Medium Protein/Small Starchy/Small Fibrous Carbohydrate
40 minutes to make
Serves at least 4 adults

Ingredients

2 large tins of tuna in brine or spring water
  (drain one tin only)
2 celery stalks, diced
1 medium onion, diced
1 large potato, diced (leave the skin on)
8 mushrooms, sliced
½ teaspoon dill
4 cups fat free chicken stock
1 small tin evaporated skim milk
salt and pepper to taste
cornflour (if needed)

Method

1 In a large saucepan, combine all the ingredients.
2 Bring to the boil, then reduce the heat. Put a lid on the saucepan and simmer for approximately 30 minutes, stirring occasionally.
3 If you wish to thicken the chowder, carefully add cornflour after you've blended it with a little water in a separate bowl.
4 If you are eating this for lunch, a great idea is to empty out some large, heavy, white-bread rolls, and pour in the chowder.

Chicken

Honey Chicken

Crumbed Chicken with Lime Sauce

Lemon Herb Chicken

Chicken in Homemade Barbecue Sauce

Chicken Cordon Bleu

Honey Chicken

B   L   D

Large Protein/Medium Carbohydrate (optional)
20 minutes to make
Serves at least 4 adults

Ingredients

2 cups quick brown rice and water for cooking
6 large chicken breast fillets (skinless and boneless)
1 large onion, chopped
1 cup fat free chicken stock
1 tablespoon parsley, freshly chopped
4 tablespoons honey

Method

1 Begin cooking rice in a large saucepan of boiling water, stirring occasionally, adding more water if necessary.
2 Chop the chicken into large, bite-sized pieces.
3 In a large non-stick frypan, cook the chicken, onion, stock, parsley and honey on medium-high heat until chicken is brown.
4 Reduce temperature and remove lid. Cook until sauce thickens slightly (a hot toffee-like consistency).
5 Turn stove off. Add a little water if sauce is too thick, and cover pan with lid.
6 Remove rice from heat and wash thoroughly using a colander.
7 Serve honey chicken on rice with a side serve of lightly steamed carrots, corn and broccoli. (No rice if you're eating this meal in the evening – serve with a crunchy green salad instead.)

Crumbed Chicken with Lime Sauce

B L D

Large Protein/Small Fibrous Carbohydrate
25 minutes to make
Serves 4 adults

Ingredients

4 large chicken breast fillets (skinless and boneless)
2 cups breadcrumbs
salt and pepper to taste
2 cups cornflour
2 teaspoons sweet paprika
2 eggs
2 tablespoons fat free chicken gravy powder
juice of 1 lime
1 cup water

Method

1 Wash chicken and remove any traces of fat.
2 Prepare 2 sheets of greaseproof paper.
3 Place breadcrumbs with salt mixed in well on one sheet, and cornflour, pepper and paprika, mixed well, on the other sheet.
4 In a small bowl, beat eggs well.
5 Roll the chicken in the cornflour, then dip in the beaten egg, then roll in the breadcrumbs.
6 Place chicken in a preheated non-stick frypan. When one side is slightly brown, turn chicken and place a lid on the pan.
7 Check carefully that the chicken has cooked through and that it has browned. Remove from the heat.
8 Add chicken gravy powder, lime juice and water (a little at a time), to a separate non-stick saucepan. Stir until thick. Pour over the crumbed chicken.
9 Serve with crunchy salad vegetables. Garnish with a slice of lime.

Lemon Herb Chicken

B L D

Large Protein/Small Fibrous Carbohydrate
15 minutes to make
Serves 4 adults

Ingredients

4 large chicken breast fillets (skinless and boneless)
2 teaspoons dried mixed herbs
½ cup fat free chicken stock
2 lemons
salt and pepper to taste

Method

1 Wash chicken and leave it in whole fillets.
2 Place in medium-sized non-stick frypan.
3 Add herbs, the juice of 1½ lemons, stock, pepper and salt.
4 Begin to cook at a medium–high temperature.
5 Place a lid on the saucepan after one side of chicken has been seared and turned over. Reduce heat slightly.
6 After a few minutes the chicken will be cooked (be careful not to overcook and dry out). Add a little more lemon if necessary.
7 Serve with a wedge of lemon and a fresh garden salad.

B L D

Chicken in Homemade Barbecue Sauce

Large Protein/Medium Fibrous/ Starchy Carbohydrate (optional)
60 minutes to make
Serves 4–6 adults

Ingredients

6 half chicken breast fillets
pepper to taste
3 teaspoons fat free chicken stock powder
1 medium onion, finely chopped
¼ cup cold water
5 tablespoons white wine
5 tablespoons soy sauce
1 heaped tablespoon tomato purée
1 heaped teaspoon mustard powder
1 teaspoon crushed garlic

Method

1 Preheat oven to 200°C (400°F).
2 Wash and dry fillets very well and slice in half. Rub each piece all over with pepper and some of the stock.
3 Place chicken into a shallow roasting pan, tucking the onion among the pieces. Sprinkle them with the remaining stock and a few drops of water.
4 Place the pan on the highest oven shelf. Cook for 30 minutes.
5 Whisk sauce ingredients until blended, then pour over the chicken. Cook for a further 25 minutes, basting frequently.
7 Serve hot with brown rice and a crisp garden salad. (No rice if eating this meal for dinner.)

B   L   D

Chicken Cordon Bleu

Large Protein/Small Fibrous Carbohydrate
25 minutes to make
Serves 4 adults

Ingredients

4 large chicken breast fillets (skinless and boneless)
2 large slices 98% fat free smoked ham (available
    from your local Deli)
2 slices 97–98% fat free cheese
8 toothpicks
1/2 cup fat free chicken stock
salt and pepper to taste

Method

1 Wash chicken and remove any traces of fat.
2 Slice chicken in half as you would a bread roll, not quite all the way through.
3 Poke in half a slice of ham and half a slice of cheese.
4 Stitch up along each side with two toothpicks per chicken breast.
5 Heat a large non-stick frypan and add half the chicken stock.
6 When stock is heated, add the chicken fillets. Keep temperature fairly high until one side is slightly browned.
7 Turn chicken over, place lid on frypan and reduce heat to low–medium. Add a little more stock if necessary.
8 Serve with steamed winter vegetables and a sprinkle of parsley. (Don't forget – no starchy carbs if you eat this meal in the evening!)

Veal

Vienna Schnitzel

Veal Stroganoff

Italian Veal Casserole

Cajun Veal Kebabs

Veal and Broccoli in Creamy Cheese Sauce

Vienna Schnitzel

B L D

Large Protein/Medium Fibrous Carbohydrate (optional)
30 minutes to make
Serves 4 adults

Ingredients

1 cup breadcrumbs
salt and pepper to taste
1 cup cornflour
1 teaspoon sweet paprika
2 eggs
2 tablespoons lemon juice
6 large, very lean veal schnitzel fillets
1 small tube of anchovy paste (optional)
fat free beef gravy powder and water
2 tablespoons lemon juice

Method

1 Prepare 2 sheets of greaseproof paper.
2 Place breadcrumbs with salt mixed in well on one sheet of greaseproof paper, and cornflour, pepper and paprika mixed well on the other.
3 In a small bowl, beat eggs with the lemon juice.
4 Coat the meat in anchovy sauce if using it. Roll meat in the cornflour. Dip it in the egg, then roll in the breadcrumbs.
5 Place the veal in a large, preheated non-stick frypan.
6 When one side of the meat has browned slightly, turn it over and place a lid on the pan.
7 It will cook quickly, so be careful not to overcook. When browned and cooked through, remove from the heat.
8 Serve with slightly steamed vegetables and a slice of lemon. If desired, also serve with gravy with a squeeze of lemon.

Veal Stroganoff

B   L   D

Large Protein/Medium Starchy Carbohydrate (optional)
20 minutes to make
Serves 4 adults

Ingredients

1 kilo very lean veal, finely diced
1/2 cup fat free chicken stock
1 cup button mushrooms
2 packets fat free stroganoff sauce packet mix
1 1/2–2 cups skim milk
salt and pepper to taste

Method

1 Lightly brown the veal in the stock in a medium–large non-stick frypan. Chop and add the button mushrooms.
2 In a small non-stick saucepan, mix the stroganoff sauce mix with milk until thickened.
3 Pour the sauce into the frypan. Reduce the sauce if necessary.
4 When the meat and sauce have browned slightly, remove from heat.
5 Serve hot over brown and wild rice. (No rice if you eat this dish in the evening.)

Italian Veal Casserole

Large Protein/Medium Fibrous Carbohydrate (optional)
40 minutes to make
Serves 4 adults

Ingredients

1 medium onion, roughly chopped
1 teaspoon crushed garlic
1 kilo very lean veal, finely diced
½ cup fat free chicken stock
275 mL white wine
350 grams tomatoes, peeled and chopped
1 tablespoon tomato paste
salt and pepper to taste
parsley and lemon rind for garnish

Method

1 In a large non-stick frypan, cook the onion and garlic in the chicken stock until golden (about 10 minutes).
2 Add the veal and brown slightly on both sides.
3 Pour in wine and let it bubble and reduce a little before adding tomatoes, tomato paste, and salt and pepper.
4 Cover the pan and allow meat to cook slowly for 20 minutes. Remove the lid and let the casserole cook gently for another 10 minutes or until the sauce has reduced.
5 Garnish with chopped parsley and lemon rind and serve with lightly steamed vegetables. (No starchy carbohydrates if you eat this meal in the evening.)

Cajun Veal Kebabs

B L D

Large Protein/Medium Starchy Carbohydrate (optional)
30 minutes to make
Serves 4 adults

Ingredients

750 grams of lean, bite-sized cubes of veal
1 cup fat free Cajun seasoning sauce
2 large onions
2 large capsicums, red and green
1 small tin unsweetened pineapple (fresh if available)
1 lemon
salt and pepper to taste
12 kebab skewers

Method

1 Marinade the veal in the Cajun sauce for half a day if possible, or for at least one hour.
2 Chop the onion and capsicums into large, bite-sized pieces.
3 Alternatively skewer the veal, onion, pineapple, capsicum, until skewer is full.
4 Using the same or a little extra Cajun sauce, continue to marinade the kebabs for approximately 20 minutes.
5 If you have the facilities, they are best barbecued. If not, cook in a very hot non-stick frypan or grill. Ensure that you don't over or undercook.
6 Serve immediately over white and wild rice with a slice of lemon. (Serve without rice if you are eating this dish in the evening.)

Veal and Broccoli in Creamy Cheese Sauce

B   L   D

Medium Protein/Small Fibrous Carbohydrate/ Medium Starchy Carbohydrate (optional)
20 minutes to make
Serves 4 adults

Ingredients

1 kilo very lean veal, finely diced
½ cup fat free chicken stock
salt and pepper to taste
1 medium onion, chopped
2 packets low fat cheese sauce packet mix
1 cup skim milk
¼ cup white wine
1 large head of broccoli chopped into small, bite-sized pieces
½ cup spring onions, finely chopped

Method

1 In a large non-stick frypan with lid on, lightly brown the veal in the stock, salt and pepper, white wine, spring onions and onion.
2 In a separate bowl, mix the cheese sauce and milk.
3 When veal is nearly cooked, add the broccoli and simmer for 5 minutes on a low heat with the lid on.
4 Add the cheese sauce mixture and stir well.
5 Allow to simmer for a further 5 minutes and let the cheese sauce go slightly brown.
6 Serve nice and hot over jasmine rice. (No rice if you eat this dish in the evening.)

Beef

Satay Beef with Fresh Garden Greens

Fillet Steak in Oyster Sauce

Pepper Steak with Dijon Mustard and Garlic

Beef Curry with Whole Spices

Baked Meatloaf with Barbecue Sauce

Satay Beef with Fresh Garden Greens B L D

Large Protein/Small Fibrous Carbohydrate/
Small Starchy Carbohydrate (optional)
20 minutes to make
Serves 4 adults

Ingredients

6 fillet steaks, 1 inch thick
1 teaspoon sweet paprika
4 tablespoons fat free satay seasoning powder
1 teaspoon salt
1 cup fat free beef stock
1 small onion, chopped
1 large head of broccoli, chopped into small, bite-sized pieces
1 tablespoon fat free beef gravy powder

Method

1 Trim the steak of all fat and cut into thin, small strips.
2 Mix the paprika and satay seasoning with the salt.
3 Rub the mixture into the meat thoroughly and leave to marinade for as long as possible.
4 Using a large non-stick frypan on a high heat, place the steak in the pan with half the stock and the onions.
5 When the steak is nearly cooked, add the broccoli.
6 Mix the beef gravy powder with the remaining stock in a separate bowl.
7 When broccoli has just softened, pour in gravy mixture.
8 Allow to simmer on a low heat for 5 minutes. Add a little water if necessary.
9 Serve with a crunchy garden salad and a small serve of rice. (Definitely no rice if you eat this meal in the evening.)

B   L   D

Fillet Steak in Oyster Sauce

Large Protein/Small Fibrous Carbohydrate/
Small Starchy Carbohydrate (optional)
25 minutes to make
Serves 4 adults

Ingredients

6 fillet steaks, 1 inch thick
1 onion, thinly sliced
$\frac{1}{2}$ cup fat free beef stock
1 cup bamboo shoots
pepper
4 tablespoons oyster sauce
1 dessertspoon soy sauce
2 cups whole baby green beans

Method

1 Remove all fat from steak and cut into thin, bite-sized strips.
2 In a large non-stick frypan, cook the steak with the onion, stock and pepper.
3 Just before steak is cooked, add the oyster sauce, bamboo shoots, beans and soy sauce.
4 Simmer for 5 minutes on a low heat, being very careful not to overcook.
5 When sauce has reduced slightly, place lid on pan and turn off heat.
6 Serve on a bed of jasmine rice with lightly steamed Chinese vegetables. (No rice if you eat this dish in the evening.)

B   L   D

Pepper Steak with Dijon Mustard and Garlic

Large Protein/Small Fibrous Carbohydrate
25 minutes to make
Serves 4 adults

Ingredients

4 fillet steaks, 1½ inches thick
2 tablespoons Dijon seed mustard (no oil)
1 teaspoon crushed garlic
2 teaspoons pepper
½ teaspoon salt
½ cup thick fat free teriyaki sauce
½ cup water

Method

1 Remove all fat from steak and place into a shallow dish to marinade with all of the other ingredients except the water.
2 In a medium, preheated non-stick frypan, sear the steak both sides then add the rest of the marinade.
3 Reduce the heat and cook until steak is done to taste.
4 Add water a little at a time only if necessary. If necessary, add a little more teriyaki sauce.
5 Serve with thinly-sliced carrots and steamed green vegetables.

Beef Curry with Whole Spices

B   L   D

Large Protein/Medium Starchy Carbohydrate (optional)
30 minutes to make (plus 2 hours simmering time)
Serves 4 adults

Ingredients

2 teaspoons coriander seeds, crushed
1 teaspoon cumin seeds, crushed
1 tablespoon turmeric
700 grams fillet steak, all fat removed, cut into strips
2 large onions, sliced
½ cup fat free beef stock
2 teaspoons crushed garlic
2 fresh capsicums, cut into strips
1 dessertspoon ground ginger
55 mL hot water
150 grams low-fat natural yoghurt
salt and pepper to taste

Method

1 Place spices in a non-stick frypan, dry-frying for 5 minutes over a gentle heat.
2 In a separate non-stick frypan, brown the meat by dry-frying and then remove to a plate.
3 Add the onions to the meat frypan and cook in beef stock for 5 minutes. Add spices, garlic and capsicum.
4 Cook for a further 5 minutes. Return meat to the pan.
5 Mix the water and yoghurt and add salt. Add to the meat. Cover the frypan and simmer for 2 hours on a low heat.
6 After 2 hours remove the lid and continue to cook for 15 minutes to reduce the sauce slightly.
7 Serve with jasmine rice and sliced fruit. (No rice in the evening!)

Baked Meatloaf with Barbecue Sauce   B   L   D

Medium Protein/Minimal Starchy Carbohydrate
60 minutes to make (including baking time)
Serves 4 adults

Ingredients

750 grams very lean minced beef
3 eggs
3 heaped tablespoons cornflour (a little extra if necessary)
2 heaped tablespoons breadcrumbs
4 tablespoons tomato paste
2 tablespoons Worcestershire sauce
2 tablespoons thick fat free teriyaki sauce
1 tablespoon seasoning sauce
1 tablespoon Italian herbs
3 teaspoons dry or 2 stalks of fresh parsley, chopped
1 large onion, chopped finely and 1 large carrot, grated finely
2 teaspoons fat free beef stock powder
2 teaspoons salt and 2 teaspoons pepper

Method

1 Preheat oven to 180°C (350°F).
2 Mix all ingredients except breadcrumbs. If mixture is too wet, keep adding cornflour.
3 Roll mixture in breadcrumbs. Work until mixture sits firm and is well covered. Sprinkle with salt and pepper.
5 Place the meatloaf on a rack and put the rack in a pan. Cover with foil. Cook in the oven (middle shelf) for 25 minutes.
6 Remove foil and continue cooking for another 25 minutes.
7 Serve with barbecue gravy: 2 tablespoons fat free beef gravy powder, 2 tablespoons tomato sauce, 1 tablespoon Worcestershire sauce and 1 cup of water, stirred in a non-stick pan on a low–medium heat. Add water if necessary.

Lamb

Roast Lamb with Rosemary

Oriental Lamb

Irish Stew with Dumplings

Lamb Curry

Lebanese Green Bean Stew

Roast Lamb with Rosemary

B   L   D

Medium Protein/Medium Fibrous/ Medium Starchy Carbohydrate
2¹/₂ hours to make (including baking time)
Serves at least 4 adults

Ingredients

1 medium lean leg of lamb
2 dessertspoons 100% fruit strawberry jam
2 teaspoons rosemary, dried, or 2 tablespoons fresh leaves
6 bay leaves
2 teaspoons salt and 1 teaspoon pepper
6 medium potatoes
1 large sweet potato
1 large parsnip
¹/₂ butternut pumpkin

Method

1 Preheat the oven to 180°C (350°F).
2 Place lamb in roasting dish with *no* oil. Spread jam over the leg. Then sprinkle with rosemary, bay leaves, salt and pepper.
3 Cook for an hour with the lid on (or less time for pink meat). Then in two separate baking dishes, spread out the washed, peeled and cut vegetables, also in *no* oil.
4 Cook for 20 minutes uncovered.
5 Add vegies to lamb. Continue cooking lamb and vegies, uncovered, for 20 minutes. Remove lamb when brown and crisp. Turn vegies over.
6 Turn oven to 220°C (425°F), to brown vegies. Turn when brown.
7 Serve with honey carrots, boiled peas, fat free beef gravy (no pan juices!) and a side salad.

B   L   D

Oriental Lamb

Medium Protein/Medium Fibrous Carbohydrate
40 minutes to make
Serves 4 adults

Ingredients

500 grams very lean strips of lamb (fillet is good)
1 large onion, finely sliced
½ cup celery, sliced
2 tablespoons water
1 cup mushrooms, sliced
2 tablespoons soy sauce
5 teaspoons cornflour
1 large clove garlic, crushed
1 punnet cherry tomatoes
2 cups snow peas
½ teaspoon fat free beef stock powder

Method

1 Using a large preheated non-stick frypan, sear the lamb then remove from heat and place onto a dish.
2 In a large saucepan, add onion, celery and water and cook on high for 10 minutes.
3 Add lamb and remaining ingredients except tomatoes and snow peas. Stir in gently.
4 Cover with a lid and simmer until meat has cooked through, approximately 10 more minutes.
5 Add snow peas and tomatoes. Cook for 5–7 minutes.
6 Drain off 1 cup of liquid into a small saucepan. Cook on high for approximately 5 minutes. Put all other ingredients in a container with the meat, ready for serving.
7 Pour the sauce over the lamb and vegetables. Serve.

Irish Stew with Dumplings

B   L   D

Medium Protein/Medium Starchy/ Small Fibrous Carbohydrate
2¹/₂ hours to make (including 2 hours simmering time)
Serves at least 4 adults

Ingredients

2 tablespoons plain flour
1 dessertspoon chicken salt
1 kilo very lean filleted lamb
1 large onion, sliced
2 large carrots, sliced
2 medium leeks, washed and sliced
salt and pepper to taste
1 large potato, peeled and sliced
1 tablespoon barley
1¹/₄ L hot water
For the dumplings:
110 grams self-raising flour
1 tablespoon fresh parsley, chopped
1 egg (you may not need all of it)

Method

1 Mix flour with chicken salt. Dip the meat in the mixture.
2 Put a layer of meat in the bottom of a large non-stick pan, with some of the onions, carrots, leeks and potatoes. Season with salt and pepper. Add more meat and continue layering the ingredients until everything is in.
3 Sprinkle the barley and pour the hot water over it. Bring to simmering point. Spoon off any 'scum' that rises to the surface, then cover the pan with a lid, reduce heat and leave to simmer for 2 hours.

4 Around 15 minutes before cooking time, make the dumplings. Mix the flour with some salt and pepper and the parsley. In a separate bowl, whisk the egg. Add in a little at a time, with some water, until the mixture has a scone-like consistency.

5 When the stew is ready, remove the meat and vegies onto a large, warm serving dish, making sure you leave all the liquid in the pan. Cover the meat with foil.

6 Add some salt and pepper to the pan juices, then bring to the boil quickly.

7 Put the dumplings in, cover and cook for 20 minutes, making sure they don't come off the boil.

8 Serve the meat with the vegies and dumplings, and pour over some of the juices from the pan.

Lamb Curry

B L D

Medium Protein/Medium Fibrous Carbohydrate
40 minutes to make (including simmering time)
Serves at least 4 adults

Ingredients

2 cups precooked very lean lamb, cubed
2 medium-sized Granny Smith apples, peeled, cored and
   finely sliced
1 small tin peeled whole tomatoes (no oil)
2 dessertspoons chutney
1 dessertspoon tomato sauce
2 teaspoons Worcestershire sauce
1 teaspoon lemon juice
$^{1}/_{2}$ teaspoon lemon rind, finely grated
2 teaspoons curry powder
1 tablespoon fat free beef gravy powder
$^{1}/_{4}$ cup cold water

Method

1 Place all ingredients except the beef gravy powder and water
   into a large non-stick frypan.
2 Simmer on low–medium heat with a lid on for 30 minutes.
3 In a separate bowl, mix the beef gravy powder and water,
   then pour into frypan, stirring constantly.
4 Replace lid and continue to simmer for another 5 minutes.
5 Serve over fluffy rice for lunch, or with a side salad if you
   are eating this meal for dinner.

Lebanese Green Bean Stew
B L D

Medium Protein/Small Fibrous Carbohydrate
2¹/₂ hours to make (including simmering time)
Serves at least 4 adults

Ingredients

500 grams green string beans
500 grams very lean lamb, cubed
several meat bones (no fat)
1¹/₂ cups onions, chopped
1¹/₂ teaspoons salt
¹/₂ teaspoon pepper
¹/₂ teaspoon mixed spices
2 tablespoons tomato paste blended with 2¹/₂ cups water
2 cloves garlic
1 teaspoon ground coriander

Method

1 String the beans. Leave whole or slice down the centre.
2 In a large non-stick frypan, simmer the meat, bones and onions.
3 Mix in the beans and fry for a few minutes.
4 Add the salt, pepper and mixed spices, then pour in the tomato paste blended with water.
5 Bring to the boil, cover and simmer slowly until the meat is very tender.
6 Crush the garlic with a pinch of salt and the coriander, and cook lightly in a small non-stick frypan, adding a sprinkle of water to stop any sticking. Cook until garlic smells sweet.
7 Stir this mixture into the cooked stew.
8 At lunch serve with Rice Pilaf. If you have this meal for dinner, serve with lightly steamed broccoli and carrots.

Pork

Sweet and Sour Pork

Spicy Grilled Pork

Pork in Black Bean Sauce

Italian Marinated Pork

Pork Chow Mein

Sweet and Sour Pork

B   L   D

Medium Protein/Small Fibrous Carbohydrate
40 minutes to make
Serves 4 adults

Ingredients

500 grams very lean fillet of pork, cut into strips
440 gram tin of unsweetened pineapple pieces (drain
    and keep juice)
1 cup bamboo shoots (optional)
1 large red capsicum, chopped
2 sticks celery, chopped
$1/2$ cup water
$1/4$ cup white wine
2 tablespoons tomato sauce
1 tablespoon cornflour
$1/2$ cup spring onions, chopped

Method

1 Sear the pork in a large non-stick frypan until just golden, then put aside.
2 Using a large saucepan, add all the ingredients except the cornflour, pineapple juice and bamboo shoots.
3 In a separate bowl, dissolve the cornflour in the pineapple juice, then add to the saucepan.
4 Half-cook the contents of the saucepan on medium heat.
5 Add the pork and the bamboo shoots and cook for a further 10 minutes with the lid on.
6 Serve over fluffy rice for lunch or on its own if you're eating this meal for dinner.

Spicy Grilled Pork

B   L   D

Medium Protein/Small Fibrous Carbohydrate
30 minutes to make (and has to be refrigerated overnight)
Serves at least 4 adults

Ingredients

400 grams natural low-fat yoghurt
¼ cup French mustard (no oil)
pinch ground allspice
salt and pepper to taste
750 grams very lean pork fillet, cubed
6 metal or 6 wooden skewers (soaked for at least 2 hours in
water)

Method

1 In a large bowl combine half the yoghurt with the mustard
and seasonings.
2 Add meat and stir well until thoroughly coated. Cover and
refrigerate overnight.
3 Thread meat onto 6 skewers and grill for 15–20 minutes.
4 In a saucepan blend the remaining yoghurt with leftover
marinade and heat gently. Make sure it doesn't boil.
5 Serve kebabs on a bed of boiled rice, covered with the
yoghurt sauce. If you're eating this meal for dinner, omit
the rice and serve with the sauce and a salad.

B L D

Pork in Black Bean Sauce

Medium Protein/Small Fibrous Carbohydrate
40 minutes to make
Serves at least 4 adults

Ingredients

500 grams very lean fillet of pork, cut into strips
3 cloves garlic, crushed
1 apple, peeled and sliced
1 medium onion, sliced
¼ cup black beans
2 tablespoons soy sauce
1 tablespoon honey
1 tablespoon sherry or dry white wine
½ cup water
salt and pepper to taste

Method

1 Place the pork in a large non-stick frypan and cook until just brown.
2 Combine all the other ingredients in a large bowl.
3 Pour over the pork and cook with the lid on for a further 30 minutes on low–medium heat.
4 Serve with rice if eating for lunch, or with some lightly steamed Asian vegetables for dinner.

B   L   D

Italian Marinated Pork

Medium Protein/Small Fibrous Carbohydrate
1 hour to make (including simmering time)
Serves at least 4 adults

Ingredients

500 grams lean pork fillet, uncut
2 large onions, finely grated
1 large clove garlic, crushed
½ cup fat free chicken stock
½ cup dry white wine
4 medium carrots, finely grated
1 cup peas
1 tin peeled whole tomatoes, drained
1 teaspoon oregano
salt and pepper to taste

Method

1 In a large non-stick frypan with the lid on, simmer the pork, onions, garlic, stock and wine.
2 After around 20 minutes, when the pork is cooked, lift the pork out onto a dish.
3 Add the other ingredients, except the peas, to the pan juices and simmer for 30 minutes with the lid on.
4 Cut the pork into 1-inch slices and return to the simmering sauce. Add the peas and continue cooking for another 10 minutes.
5 Serve hot with lightly steamed green vegetables.

B L D

Pork Chow Mein

Medium Protein/Small Starchy/ Small Fibrous Carbohydrate
45 minutes to make
Serves at least 4 adults

Ingredients

500 grams very lean pork mince
1 onion, finely chopped
1 cup cooked white rice
2½ cups of water
1 tablespoon fat free chicken stock powder
½ cup rice noodles, no oil
1 tablespoon curry powder
¼ cup finely chopped spring onions
4 cups finely shredded cabbage
440 gram tin pineapple pieces, drained
¼ cup freshly chopped chives

Method

1 Combine all the ingredients except the cabbage, pineapple and chives, in a large non-stick frypan.
2 Stir well until pork is cooked thoroughly, then add the cabbage and pineapple.
3 Cook for a further 15 minutes or so, or until the noodles and all other ingredients are soft. Sprinkle chives on top.
4 Serve hot with a crusty bread roll for lunch, or on Junk Day in a large lettuce cup for dinner.

Vegetarian

Vegetable Soup

Stuffed Zucchini

Lentil and Vegetable Moussaka

Vegetarian Shepherd's Pie

Rice Pilaf

Vegetable Soup

B   L   D

Small Protein/Medium Fibrous Carbohydrate
2 hours to make (including simmering time)
Serves at least 4 adults

Ingredients

1 large onion, chopped
1 large clove garlic, crushed
2 tablespoons soy sauce
1 cup lentils
4 cups water
2 teaspoons fat free chicken stock powder
3 medium carrots, chopped
2 celery stalks, chopped
1 cup cauliflower
2 teaspoons fresh coriander, chopped
salt and pepper to taste
2 teaspoons curry powder (or to taste)
1 cup evaporated skim milk

Method

1 In a large saucepan, sauté the onion and garlic in soy sauce.
2 Soak the lentils in water for 10 minutes.
3 Add all ingredients except curry powder and evaporated milk.
4 Simmer for 90 minutes on a very low heat.
5 When completely mushy, blend.
6 Add evaporated milk, curry powder and coriander.
7 Serve piping hot with crunchy side salad. Add a bread roll if you're eating this meal for lunch.

Stuffed Zucchini   B L D

Medium Protein/Medium Fibrous Carbohydrate
60 minutes to make
Serves 4 adults

Ingredients

4 large zucchini
1/2 cup fat free vegetable stock
250 grams mushrooms, finely chopped
1 medium onion, roughly chopped
2 medium tomatoes, roughly chopped
1 celery stalk, sliced
1/2 teaspoon sweet paprika
salt and pepper to taste

Method

1 Slice the zucchini in half lengthways and scoop out the seeds and flesh.
2 In a large non-stick frypan, heat the stock until simmering. Add the mushrooms and cook until lightly browned.
3 Add the remaining ingredients and simmer for 5 minutes.
4 Spoon the mixture into the zucchini shells and place them on a non-stick baking tray.
5 Bake at 200°C (400°F) for 45 minutes, or until tender.

Lentil and Vegetable Moussaka

B   L   D

Small Protein/Medium Fibrous Carbohydrate
60 minutes to make
Serves 4 adults

Ingredients

50 grams whole green or brown lentils
110 mL water
1 medium eggplant, cut into small cubes
1½ cups fat free vegetable stock
1 large onion, finely chopped
110 grams red capsicum, finely chopped
1 large clove garlic, crushed
4 tablespoons red wine
1 tablespoon tomato purée
¼ teaspoon ground cinnamon
1 dessertspoon chopped parsley
salt and pepper to taste
For the Topping:
2 eggs (only 1 yolk)
4 tablespoons natural, low-fat yoghurt
2 teaspoons grated parmesan cheese
¼ teaspoon ground nutmeg

Method

1 Soften the lentils in the water (no salt).
2 Preheat the oven to 180°C (350°F).
3 Prepare the eggplant cubes. Place them in a colander, sprinkle them with salt and cover with a plate weighed down with a heavy object. Leave them to bleed for 20 minutes or so, then rinse and squeeze them dry in a clean tea towel.

4 Pour half the stock into a medium-sized non-stick frypan and cook the onion and capsicum until softened (around 10 minutes).

5 Remove them and place on a plate.

6 Using the remaining stock, cook the eggplant in the same frypan. It will take around 10 minutes to soften.

7 Add the capsicum, and cook for a minute, then add the onion and garlic.

8 In a separate bowl, mix the wine and tomato purée with the cinnamon and parsley. Pour this into the vegetable mixture. Stir in the softened lentils, and add salt and pepper.

9 Stir and combine thoroughly, then spoon everything into an ovenproof dish.

10 Beat all the topping ingredients in a separate bowl.

11 Pour topping mixture over the vegetables.

12 Bake in the oven for 30 minutes or until the top is puffy and golden.

B L D

Vegetarian Shepherd's Pie

Medium Protein/Medium Starchy/Small Fibrous Carbohydrate
90 minutes to make
Serves 4 adults

Ingredients

175 grams whole brown or green lentils
110 grams split green or yellow peas
575 mL hot water
1 cup fat free vegetable stock
2 celery stalks, chopped
1 medium onion, chopped
2 medium carrots, chopped
1/2 medium green capsicum, chopped
1 large clove garlic, crushed
1/2 teaspoon dried mixed herbs
1/4 teaspoon cayenne pepper
salt and pepper to taste
1 small tin peeled whole tomatoes
For the Topping:
1 small onion, chopped
1/2 cup fat free vegetable stock
700 grams boiled potatoes
2 tablespoons skim milk
2 teaspoons parmesan cheese, grated

Method

1 Wash then simmer the lentils and split peas in a large, covered saucepan for around 45–60 minutes, or until the peas and lentils have absorbed the water and are soft.

2 Preheat the oven to 190°C (375°C).

3 Simmer the stock in a large non-stick pan. Add the celery, onion, carrots and capsicum. Cook gently until softened, adding a little more water if necessary.

4 Mash a little. Add to lentil mixture. Then add the garlic, herbs, spices, salt and pepper. Spoon the mixture into a large pie dish. Arrange the sliced tomatoes on top.

5 For the topping, sauté the onion in the stock in a small non-stick frypan.

6 Mash the potatoes, then add the cooked onion, milk and parmesan cheese, and mix well.

7 Season with salt and pepper, then spread on top of the ingredients in the pie dish.

8 Bake for about 20 minutes or until the top is lightly browned.

9 Serve with some tomato sauce or appropriate chutney and a light crunchy green salad, with a no oil dressing.

Rice Pilaf

B   L   D

Medium Protein/Medium Starchy Carbohydrate
60 minutes to make
Serves 6–8 adults

Ingredients

1³/₄ cups lentils and water for boiling
2 large onions
¹/₂ cup fat free vegetable stock
2 cups rice, washed and drained
1 tablespoon salt
soy sauce to taste

Method

1 Wash the lentils well.
2 Slice onions into fine half-circles.
3 Toss into a hot, medium-sized non-stick frypan, and keep tossing until golden brown. Splash drops of stock to help the onions brown, but be careful not to add too much water.
4 Remove half the onions from the pan and place on a side plate.
5 In a large saucepan, boil the lentils in water until nearly tender, approximately 20–25 minutes.
6 Mix in the rice and bring back to the boil.
7 Reheat the remaining stock until really hot, then toss in the remaining onions. Pour them onto the boiling lentils and rice.
8 Add salt, cover tightly, turn down the heat and simmer slowly until the rice is tender and all the fluid is absorbed, approximately 20 minutes.
9 Serve hot or cold, garnished with the golden brown onion slices. If served cold, accompany with a tossed salad. Add a little soy sauce for a slightly salty taste.

Kids' Meals

recommended by kids!

Hamburgers

Macaroni Cheese

Kids' Spaghetti

Crumbed Fish Fillets

Colourful Chicken Kebabs

Hamburgers

Medium Protein/Small Starchy/ Small Fibrous Carbohydrate
20 minutes to make
Serves 4 kids

Ingredients

200 grams very lean beef, minced
1 small onion
1 medium tomato
some interesting lettuce (raddichio, butter, cos)
4 slices beetroot
tomato sauce
4 hamburger buns

Method

1 Heat a large non-stick frypan on high.
2 Make the mince into four even patties and put them into the pan.
3 Cut the onion into 3 mm slices, but do not separate rings.
4 Cook them in the pan with the mince.
5 Turn the patties after 5–7 minutes.
6 Split and toast the hamburger buns.
7 When patties are cooked, remove and place neatly on half of the bun. Top with onion rings.
8 Add the salad and tomato sauce.
9 Serve straightaway with Cajun Baked Sweet Potato Chips (see p. 266).

Macaroni Cheese

B L D

Large Starchy Carbohydrate
20 minutes to make
Serves 4 kids

Ingredients

2 cups uncooked macaroni elbows or bowties
4 cups water
pinch salt
2 packets 97–98% fat free cheese sauce packet mix
skim milk (as directed on back of the packet, plus a little extra)

Method

1 Using a medium-sized saucepan, cook the macaroni in slightly salted water.
2 In a small non-stick saucepan, mix the cheese sauce with milk as directed on packet.
3 Keep adding milk as you need it. Make sure the sauce isn't too thick.
4 When macaroni is cooked, after 15 minutes, remove from heat, drain and rinse well.
5 Empty macaroni into a dish and pour the cheese sauce over.

B   L   D

Kids' Spaghetti

Medium Protein/Medium Starchy/Small Fibrous Carbohydrate
60 minutes to make
Serves 4 kids

Ingredients

¼ packet thin spaghetti noodles (or any other interesting
    type of pasta)
4 cups water
pinch salt
250 grams very lean beef, minced
1 small tin whole peeled tomatoes (no oil added)
2 teaspoons mixed herbs
1 teaspoon fat free beef stock powder

Method

1 Using a large frypan, cook the mince.
2 Add tomatoes, stock and herbs.
3 Reduce heat to very low, place a lid on the frypan, and leave
   simmering for 45 minutes.
4 When the sauce is nearly ready, cook the spaghetti noodles
   in a large saucepan filled with slightly salty water.
5 When spaghetti is cooked (after 15 minutes), remove from
   heat, drain and rinse well.
6 Empty into a serving dish. Pour sauce over and mix in.
7 Serve hot with a small, simple salad of lettuce, carrots and
   tomato, with some Italian bread.

Crumbed Fish Fillets

B   L   D

Large Protein/Small Starchy Carbohydrate
20 minutes to make
Serves 4 kids

Ingredients

4 medium white fish fillets (as boneless as possible)
1 cup cornflour
1 cup breadcrumbs
2 eggs
salt and pepper to taste
4 small lemon wedges

Method

1 Wash the fillets well.
2 Preheat a large non-stick frypan on high.
3 Prepare 2 pieces of greaseproof paper, 1 with cornflour, the other with breadcrumbs.
4 Whisk eggs with salt and pepper to taste, in a small bowl.
5 Roll fillets in the cornflour, then dip well in the egg mixture then roll straight in the breadcrumbs.
6 Place fillets in the hot frypan, watching carefully that they don't burn. Reduce the heat immediately, and place the lid on top.
7 After a couple of minutes, turn fillets over very carefully with a spatula and keep cooking until brown.
8 Sprinkle in a little water, for extra moisture, which also helps the fish to brown slightly.
9 Serve hot with some Creamy Mashed Potatoes (see p. 269), steamed fibrous vegetables, and a lemon wedge on the side.

Colourful Chicken Kebabs B L D

Medium Protein/Medium Fibrous Carbohydrate
20 minutes to make
Serves 4 kids

Ingredients

½ cup oyster sauce
3 single chicken breast fillets
1 large carrot
2 pineapple rings
½ small green capsicum
1 small tomato
8 kebab skewers

Method

1 Wash and trim the chicken of all fat, and cut into bite-sized cubes.
2 Marinate the chicken in the oyster sauce for around 10 minutes.
3 Cut all the fruit and vegetables into bite-sized pieces.
4 Heat a large non-stick frypan, or a grill or barbeque, on high.
5 Place all the bite-sized pieces, including the chicken, on the kebabs, to make them colourful and interesting.
6 When the pan is hot, toss in the kebabs, four at a time. Turn them as they cook.
7 Remove when cooked and serve with a crunchy salad.

Soups

Pumpkin, Parsnip and Tomato

Chicken and Corn

Leek, Onion and Potato

Minestrone

Homestyle Beef and Vegetable

Pumpkin, Parsnip and Tomato Soup   B L D

Medium Fibrous/Small Starchy Carbohydrate
25 minutes to make
Serves 4 adults

Ingredients

1 medium–large parsnip
½ butternut pumpkin
4 ripe tomatoes
1 teaspoon dried mixed herbs
1 teaspoon fat free vegetable stock powder
salt and pepper to taste
a little low-fat sour cream (only if it's Junk Day)
fresh chives, finely chopped, for garnish

Method

1 Remove skin from pumpkin and parsnip.
2 Chop pumpkin, parsnip and tomatoes into chunks.
3 Steam the pumpkin and parsnip in a large saucepan.
4 When cooked, place all ingredients into a large saucepan with 2 tablespoons of water.
5 Simmer on a very low temperature until the tomatoes are cooked.
6 Blend all the ingredients until it reaches a soup consistency.
7 If you've been good all week, you may add two teaspoons of low-fat sour cream or yoghurt and a sprinkle of chives.
8 Serve with a hot crunchy bread roll (no butter).

Chicken and Corn Soup

B   L   D

Medium Protein/Small Fibrous Carbohydrate
50 minutes to make
Makes 10–12 servings

Ingredients

6 half chicken breast fillets, finely chopped
10 cups water
1 small onion, roughly chopped
2 slices 98% fat free smoked ham, finely chopped
1 knot root ginger (about 1 inch long), finely chopped
6 large stalks spring onions, finely chopped
1 large tin corn kernels
3 tablespoons cornflour
⅓ cup water
2 teaspoons soy sauce
1 egg

Method

1 Place chicken in a large saucepan with the water.
2 Bring to the boil and simmer on a low heat for approximately 40 minutes or until chicken is cooked.
3 Add all other ingredients except cornflour, water, soy sauce and egg. Bring to the boil.
4 In a small container, mix cornflour and water to a smooth paste, add to soup and let simmer, stirring for 3 minutes.
5 Add soy sauce.
6 In a small container, beat the egg lightly with a fork, then stir into the soup.
7 Serve piping hot with a sprinkle of salt and pepper.

B   L   D

Leek, Onion and Potato Soup

Small Fibrous/Medium Starchy Carbohydrate
45 minutes to make
Makes 4–6 servings

Ingredients

4 large leeks
2 medium potatoes, peeled and diced
1 medium onion, finely chopped
2 teaspoons fresh chives, finely chopped
1 teaspoon fat free vegetable stock powder
1 L water
salt and pepper to taste
325 mL skim milk

Method

1 Remove outer layer of leeks, chop finely, wash thoroughly and drain well.
2 In a large saucepan, add leeks, potatoes, onion, stock, and half a cup of water. Stir with a wooden spoon so everything is coated with the chicken stock.
3 Add salt and pepper, then cover and let the vegetables sweat over a very low heat for 15 minutes.
4 Add the stock and milk, bring to simmering point, put the lid back on and let the soup simmer very gently for a further 20 minutes or until the vegetables are very soft. Be careful not to overheat or boil over.
5 If you don't like chunky soup, use a liquidiser to purée the ingredients.
6 Stir in chopped chives and serve nice and hot with a fresh bread roll.

Minestrone Soup

B   L   D

Small Protein/Medium Fibrous/
Medium Starchy Carbohydrate
45 minutes to make
Makes 10–12 servings

Ingredients

2 potatoes with the skin on, roughly chopped
4 carrots, peeled and finely sliced
3 onions, roughly chopped
1 teaspoon crushed garlic
1 medium tin red kidney beans (no oil)
½ cup fat free chicken stock
14 cups fat free beef stock (6 teaspoons stock and 14 cups hot water)
1 large tin peeled tomatoes
4 celery stalks, finely sliced
3 slices 98% fat free smoked ham, roughly chopped
1 cup macaroni
1 tablespoon chopped parsley
1 dessertspoon freshly chopped basil
salt and pepper to taste

Method

1 Sauté the vegetables and ham with the chicken stock in a large saucepan. Add beef stock, beans and tomatoes.
2 Bring to the boil, cover and simmer for 30 minutes.
3 Add macaroni and simmer uncovered, until tender.
4 Serve with a sprinkle of parsley and salt and pepper.

Homestyle Beef and Vegetable Soup   B   L   D

Medium Protein/Medium Fibrous Carbohydrate
Make overnight
Makes 10–12 servings

Ingredients

1 L fat free beef stock
1 cup barley
1 kilo very lean beef, cubed
4 carrots, roughly grated
2 turnips, roughly grated
1 small swede, roughly grated
1 large leek, roughly chopped
1 cup chopped celery
½ cup fresh parsley, finely chopped

Method

1 In a really large cooking pot, place all the ingredients.
2 Cook for 1–1½ hours or until the meat is tender.
3 Leave overnight for fat to set. It will do this best in the fridge.
4 Skim any fat off the top of the soup the next morning.
5 Add more beef stock if necessary, and simmer for another hour, or until barley is nice and soft.
6 Serve piping hot with a crunchy roll – no butter!

Salads

Italian Tomato

Coleslaw

Chinese Greens

Waldorf

Tabbouleh

B   L   D

Italian Tomato Salad

Large Fibrous Carbohydrate
10 minutes to make
Serves 2 adults

Ingredients

2 large tomatoes, sliced
2 large zucchini, sliced
1 large Spanish onion, sliced
a few fresh basil leaves
salt and pepper to taste
¾ cup fat free Italian dressing

Method

1 Using a glass salad bowl, alternately layer all the vegetables and basil leaves.
2 Pour the salad dressing over everything.
3 Add salt and pepper to taste.
4 Serve on its own or to accompany another dish.

B   L   D

Coleslaw

Large Fibrous Carbohydrate
15 minutes to make
Serves 4 adults

Ingredients

½ cup carrots, shredded
¼ cup white onion, finely chopped
1 cup mixed red and green cabbage, shredded
2 teaspoons parsley, finely chopped
¼ cup brown vinegar
¼ cup Italian dressing (no oil)
1 dessertspoon honey
sprinkle pepper

Method

1 Combine vegetables in a large mixing bowl.
2 Mix vinegar, dressing, honey and pepper in a separate, smaller bowl.
3 Pour liquid ingredients over vegetables and mix well.
4 Cover and chill.
5 Serve as an accompaniment to another dish.

B L D

Chinese Greens

Large Fibrous Carbohydrate
10 minutes to make
Serves 4 adults

Ingredients

2 cups chopped Chinese green vegetables
2 cups fresh baby spinach leaves
1 cup fresh bamboo shoots
1 cup thinly sliced radishes
½ cup chopped mushrooms
1 punnet cherry tomatoes
¼ cup Italian dressing (no oil)
1 tablespoon honey
2 tablespoons soy sauce
pepper to taste

Method

1 Thoroughly wash and drain all green vegetables, remove all stems, then place in large glass salad bowl.
2 Add radishes, mushrooms, tomatoes and bamboo shoots.
3 Mix dressing, honey, soy sauce and pepper in small bowl.
4 Pour dressing over salad and toss well.

B   L   D

Waldorf Salad

Large Fibrous Carbohydrate
10 minutes to make
Serves 4 adults

Ingredients

1 tablespoon of lemon juice
3 large red apples, washed and diced
1½ cups celery, washed and diced, unstrung
¼ cup raisins
1 low fat vanilla flavoured yoghurt
parsley for garnish

Method

1 Place apples in a medium-sized glass salad bowl.
2 Squeeze lemon juice over apples to prevent discolouring.
3 Add remaining ingredients and toss well.
4 Cover and chill before serving.

B   L   D

Tabbouleh

Medium Fibrous Carbohydrate
1¹/₂ hours to make
Serves 4 adults

Ingredients

¹/₂ cup instant burghul (cracked wheat)
8–10 spring onions
2 teaspoons salt
¹/₄ teaspoon pepper
¹/₄ teaspoon mixed spices
5 cups very finely chopped parsley
¹/₄ cup very finely chopped fresh mint *or* 2 teaspoons dried mint
3 large tomatoes, finely chopped
¹/₄ cup lemon juice
¹/₄ cup fat free Mediterranean salad dressing

Method

1 Wash the burghul and drain well by squeezing out excess water with cupped hands.
2 Place in a bowl and refrigerate for at least 1 hour.
3 Trim the spring onions, leaving about 20 cm of green.
4 Finely chop the white of the spring onions and mix it into the drained burghul with the salt, pepper and spices.
5 Finely chop the green of the spring onions and place it with parsley, mint and tomatoes on top of the burghul mixture. Set aside in the refrigerator until ready to serve.
6 Just before serving, add the lemon juice and dressing and toss well. Add salt and lemon juice to taste.

Vegetables

Honey Carrots

Super Stir Fry

Corn and Sweet Potato Mash

Barbecued Italian Peppers

Ratatouille

B L D

Honey Carrots

Medium Fibrous Carbohydrate
15 minutes to make
Serves 4 adults

Ingredients

1 cup water
8 medium carrots, peeled and cut diagonally, 1cm thick
$3/4$ teaspoon ground cumin
$1/2$ teaspoon fresh ginger, crushed
$1/4$ teaspoon ground coriander
$1/8$ teaspoon cayenne pepper
2 tablespoons honey
2 teaspoons lemon juice

Method

1 Using a medium-sized saucepan, boil water.
2 When boiling, add everything except honey and lemon juice.
3 Reduce the heat and simmer for 5 minutes.
4 Add lemon juice and honey.
5 Turn up heat and cook until all liquid has evaporated and carrots are soft (around 5 minutes). Drain and serve.

Super Stir Fry

B   L   D

Large Fibrous Carbohydrate
15 minutes to make
Serves 4 adults

Ingredients

1 medium head of broccoli
1 small head cauliflower
$\frac{1}{2}$ red pepper
1 cup snow peas
1 large zucchini, sliced in chunks
2 large carrots, finely sliced
1 medium Spanish onion, finely sliced
1 cup shredded red and white cabbage
$\frac{1}{2}$ cup oyster sauce

Method

1 Wash broccoli and cauliflower and prepare into small, bite-sized pieces.
2 Preheat a large non-stick frypan on high then add all the ingredients. Cover with lid.
3 Cook for a couple of minutes, and stir well.
4 After another 5 minutes with the lid on, remove from heat and serve.

Corn and Sweet Potato Mash

Medium Starchy/Medium Fibrous Carbohydrate
30 minutes to make
Serves 4 adults

Ingredients

1 large sweet potato, washed and peeled
2 large potatoes, washed and peeled
1 large tin corn kernels
salt and pepper to taste
fresh parsley

Method

1 Steam the potatoes until soft over a little water in a large saucepan, approximately 15–20 minutes.
2 Drain the corn well.
3 Place the potato and corn in a medium-sized mixing bowl.
4 Using a blender, whip up the vegetables, adding salt and pepper to taste.
5 Garnish with parsley.

Barbecued Italian Peppers

B L D

Medium Fibrous Carbohydrate
20 minutes to make
Serves 4 adults

Ingredients

4 large red capsicums, washed
1 cup red wine vinegar
2 tablespoons fresh basil, chopped
salt and pepper to taste

Method

1 Preheat an outdoor barbecue or an indoor health grill until very hot.
2 Place capsicums on grill and turn. Continue turning until skin has blistered and blackened on all sides.
3 Remove and place in a bowl of cold salty water to loosen skins. Carefully remove skins.
4 After removing skins, place in a shallow serving dish.
5 Pour over vinegar, salt and pepper, and sprinkle with basil.
6 Cover and chill.

B   L   D

Ratatouille

Medium Fibrous Carbohydrate
30 minutes to make
Serves 4 adults

Ingredients

2 large eggplants
3 medium zucchini
1 red and 1 green capsicum, cored, deseeded and chopped
1 large tin whole peeled tomatoes (no oil), chopped
1 tablespoon fresh basil *or* 2 teaspoons dried basil
³/₄ cup fat free vegetable stock
2 large cloves garlic, crushed
2 medium onions, roughly chopped
salt and pepper to taste
fresh basil leaves or parsley to garnish

Method

1 Wipe eggplant, cut into 1 inch slices, then halve each slice.
2 Wipe zucchini and cut into 1 inch slices.
3 Put eggplant and zucchini into a colander. Sprinkle generously with salt. Press them down with a plate. Let stand for 1 hour.
4 In a medium non-stick frypan, heat the stock. Add onion and garlic. Cook for 10 minutes then add capsicum.
5 Dry zucchini and eggplant in a towel, then add to the pan.
6 Add the basil, salt and pepper. Stir once really well. Simmer very gently with the lid on for around 30 minutes.
7 Now add the tomato. Taste to make sure the seasoning is right. Cook for a further 10 minutes or so with the lid off.
8 Serve hot as a side dish, with a garnish of fresh basil leaves.

Potatoes

Summer Potato Salad

Cajun Baked Sweet Potato Chips

Potatoes au Gratin

Chipped Potato Grits

Creamy Mashed Potatoes

Summer Potato Salad

B L D

Small Protein/Large Carbohydrate
30 minutes to make
Serves 4 adults

Ingredients

1 kilo Pontiac potatoes, washed and cut into small cubes
(leave skin on)
4 eggs, boiled and roughly chopped
½ cup finely chopped fresh parsley
½ cup finely chopped fresh chives
1 large stalk of celery, finely chopped
1 large onion, finely chopped
1 cup low-fat natural yoghurt
2 tablespoons fat free Italian salad dressing
2 tablespoons fat free mayonnaise
1 teaspoon mustard powder
½ teaspoon salt
½ teaspoon pepper

Method

1 Parboil the potatoes, being careful not to cook them until
they're mushy.
2 Combine all the other ingredients in a mixing bowl and stir well.
3 Place potatoes in a serving dish and add the dressing.
4 Mix and refrigerate.
5 Best served cold.

Cajun Baked Sweet Potato Chips

B L D

Medium Starchy Carbohydrate
30 minutes to make
Serves 4 adults

Ingredients

1 kilo sweet potatoes, washed and cut into chip strips
   (or substitute Pontiac potatoes with skin left on)
3 eggs
salt and pepper to taste
1 small jar Cajun spices

Method

1 Preheat oven to 220°C (425°F).
2 Beat eggs with salt, pepper and Cajun spices.
3 Dip potato chip strips in egg mixture then place on a non-stick tray and place in the oven to bake for 15 minutes.
4 Check them. When they're brown on one side, turn them, adding a little more Cajun spices and salt.
5 When they're cooked through, after about another 15 minutes, remove from oven.
6 Serve and eat straightaway.

B   L   D

Potatoes au Gratin

Large Starchy Carbohydrate
60 minutes to make
Serves 4 adults

Ingredients

1 kilo Pontiac potatoes, washed and cut into very thin slices
   (leave skin on)
2 extra-large onions, cut into fine rings
¼ cup finely chopped fresh spring onions
1 packet fat free cheese sauce mix
750 mL skim milk
4 slices 98% fat free ham, finely chopped
salt and pepper to taste
1 teaspoon sweet paprika
½ teaspoon crushed garlic

Method

1 Preheat the oven to 205°C (400°F).
2 In a large, ovenproof casserole dish, place the potato slices
   and onion rings and mix well with the ham and spring onions.
3 Mix cheese sauce, milk and other ingredients in a separate bowl.
4 Pour sauce over the potato mixture.
5 Place in the oven until potatoes are browned slightly and
   soft, approximately 60 minutes.

Chipped Potato Grits

B   L   D

Large Starchy Carbohydrate
20 minutes to make
Serves 4 adults

Ingredients

- 1 kilo Pontiac potatoes, washed and cut into very thin slices (leave skin on)
- 2 extra-large onions, cut into fine rings
- 1 teaspoon dried dill
- 2 cups fat free vegetable stock

Method

1 Place all ingredients in a large non-stick frypan and cover.
2 Allow to cook on a medium-high heat until potatoes are soft.
3 Reduce the heat and allow to simmer while fluids reduce.
4 Add a little water as you go if necessary.
5 Stir so it looks really messy.

B   L   D

Creamy Mashed Potatoes

Large Starchy Carbohydrate
15 minutes to make
Serves 4 adults

Ingredients

1 kilo Pontiac potatoes, cut into quarters (leave skin on)
1 egg
a little skim milk
salt and pepper to taste
¼ cup freshly chopped parsley

Method

1. Boil the potatoes until soft.
2. Drain well and place in bowl ready for mixing.
3. In a separate bowl, whisk the egg.
4. Mash the potatoes dry at first, adding the egg. Then, using an electric mixer, give the potatoes a good mash.
5. Add a little skim milk until the mixture is nice and creamy. Be careful not to add too much. If you do, put in a saucepan on the stove on a medium heat until reduced a little.
6. Add salt and pepper to taste and garnish with parsley.

Pasta

Spaghetti Bolognaise

Fettucine Boscaiola

Fettucine Salmone

Gnocchi with Crabmeat

Tortellini with Chicken and Mushrooms

B L D

Spaghetti Bolognaise

Medium Protein/Large Starchy Carbohydrate
20 minutes to make
Serves at least 4 adults

Ingredients

1 packet spaghetti and water for boiling
500 grams lean beef mince
1 medium onion, chopped
1 cup fat free beef stock
¼ cup red wine
3 teaspoons dried Italian herbs
1 teaspoon paprika
1 teaspoon crushed garlic
2 tablespoons fat free beef gravy powder
1 cup water
250 grams tomato paste
325 grams tomato soup
325 grams whole peeled tomatoes

Method

1 Begin cooking spaghetti in a large saucepan of boiling water, stirring occasionally. Add more water if necessary.
2 In a large non-stick frypan, cook the beef, onion, stock and wine on medium–high heat until brown.
3 Turn down heat and add herbs, garlic, tomato paste, tomato puree and whole tomatoes. Stir.
4 In a separate bowl, mix the beef gravy powder with 1 cup of water and slowly add to the other ingredients.
6 Turn off stove and cover frypan with a lid.
7 Drain spaghetti and wash thoroughly using a colander.
8 Serve bolognaise sauce on spaghetti piping hot, with a side serve of salad vegetables.

Fettuccine Boscaiola

B L D

Small Protein/Large Starchy Carbohydrate
25 minutes to make
Serves at least 4 adults

Ingredients

1 large packet fettuccine and water for boiling
1 large onion, finely chopped
3 large spring onion stalks, finely chopped
4 slices 98% fat free smoked ham, finely chopped
1 cup button mushrooms, finely chopped
½ cup fat free chicken stock
1 teaspoon dried or fresh parsley
salt and pepper to taste
2 packets 97–98% fat free cheese sauce packet mix
750 mL skim milk

Method

1 Cook fettuccine in a large saucepan of boiling water, stirring occasionally. Add more water if necessary. Remove from stove before noodles are too soft.

2 In a large non-stick frypan, cook onion, spring onions, ham, mushrooms, stock and parsley on medium high until browned. Add a little water if necessary. Remove from stove.

3 In a non-stick saucepan, add cheese sauce and half the milk.

4 Stir constantly until sauce thickens, then add the remaining milk until a pancake-type consistency is reached.

5 Drain and rinse fettuccine and return to large saucepan.

6 Add ingredients from the frypan, then add cheese sauce. Mix well and transfer to container for serving.

7 Allow to sit. Add more milk, if necessary, as sauce thickens.

8 Serve piping hot with a crunchy Italian roll (no butter!).

B L D

Fettuccine Salmone

Small Protein/Large Starchy Carbohydrate
25 minutes to make
Serves at least 4 adults

Ingredients

1 large packet fettuccine and water for boiling
1 large onion, finely chopped
3 large spring onion stalks, finely chopped
4 slices 98% fat free smoked ham, chopped
½ cup fat free chicken stock
2 packets 97–98% fat free cheese sauce packet mix
1 teaspoon dried or fresh parsley
1 teaspoon Italian herbs
1 teaspoon pepper
pinch of salt
100 grams smoked salmon, cut into 1 cm strips
½ cup fat free thousand island dressing
2 tablespoons tomato sauce
1 cup button mushrooms, finely chopped
750 mL skim milk

Method

1 Begin cooking fettuccine in a large saucepan of boiling water, stirring occasionally. Add more water if necessary. Remove from stove before noodles are too soft.

2 In a large non-stick frypan, cook the onion, spring onions, ham, mushrooms, stock and parsley on medium–high until browned. Add a little water if necessary. Remove from the stove.

3 Pour the cheese sauce mix and half of the milk into a small non-stick saucepan.

4 Stir constantly until sauce thickens, then add the remaining milk until a pancake-type consistency is reached.

5 Drain and rinse fettuccine and return to large saucepan.

6 Add the ingredients from the frypan. Add the cheese sauce, salmon, dressing, tomato sauce and mixed herbs.

7 Mix well and transfer to container for serving.

8 Allow to sit. Add more milk if necessary as starch begins to thicken sauce.

9 Serve piping hot with a crunchy Italian bread roll (no butter).

B L D

Gnocchi with Crabmeat

Small Protein/Large Starchy Carbohydrate
25 minutes to make
Serves at least 4 adults

Ingredients

1 packet fresh pumpkin or potato gnocchi
1 packet 97–98% fat free cheese sauce packet mix
325 mL skim milk
pinch salt
1 teaspoon pepper
1 large can white crabmeat (fresh if available)
1 teaspoon dried or fresh parsley

Method

1 Boil water in a large saucepan, then add the gnocchi. Cook for 5 minutes on high. Ensure you don't overcook. Drain then wash with cold water.

2 In a small non-stick saucepan, add the cheese sauce mix, milk, salt and pepper.

3 Stir constantly until sauce thickens, adding more milk if necessary.

4 Add the crabmeat to the cooked and thickened cheese sauce, stirring well.

5 Place the gnocchi in a serving dish. Pour the crabmeat and cheese sauce over gnocchi and mix well.

6 Allow to sit. Add more milk if necessary as starch begins to thicken.

7 Garnish with parsley and serve piping hot.

Tortellini with Chicken and Mushrooms

B L D

Medium Protein/Large Starchy Carbohydrate
25 minutes to make
Serves at least 4 adults

Ingredients

1 packet fresh low fat tortellini (no oil added)
6 half chicken breast fillets, cut into bite-sized pieces
1 medium onion, finely chopped
4 large fresh spring onion stalks, finely chopped
4 slices 98% fat free smoked ham
½ cup fat free chicken stock
1 teaspoon dried or fresh parsley
1 dessertspoon Dijon seed mustard (no oil)
1 cup button mushrooms, finely chopped
1 teaspoon pepper
large pinch salt
1 packet 97–98% fat free cheese sauce packet mix
1 packet fat free stroganoff sauce mix
750 mL skim milk

Method

1 Boil water in a large saucepan. Add pasta, and cook for 5–7 minutes on high. Don't overcook. When you drain pasta, rinse with cold water.

2 In a large non-stick frypan, cook the chicken, onion, spring onions, ham, mushrooms, stock, parsley and mustard on medium–high until browned. Add a little water if necessary, and remove from the stove.

4 Place the cheese and stroganoff mixes and half of the milk in a small non-stick saucepan.

5 Stir constantly until sauce thickens, then add the remaining milk until a pancake-type consistency is reached.

6 Add the sauce and pasta to the large frypan, mixing in well.

7 Once heated through, transfer to a suitable dish for serving.

8 Allow to sit. Add a little more milk if necessary as starch begins to thicken.

9 Serve piping hot with steamed vegetables.

Rice

Combination Fried Rice

Mexican Rice

Rice on the Side

Japanese Rice (Chirashi Zushi)

Rice Pudding

B   L   D

Combination Fried Rice

Small Protein/Large Starchy Carbohydrate
45 minutes to make
Makes 6–8 servings

Ingredients

1 kilo white rice (or brown if you prefer)
½ cup fat free chicken stock
4 slices 98% fat free ham, finely chopped
1 large onion, finely chopped
¾ cup finely chopped spring onions
2 eggs, beaten
¼ cup soy sauce
salt and pepper to taste

Method

1 Boil the rice until just cooked.
2 Wash rice thoroughly in a large colander then leave to dry for about half an hour.
3 In a large non-stick frypan, add the stock, ham, onion and spring onions and cook until brown. Add a little extra stock if necessary.
4 In a small non-stick frypan, add the eggs with soy sauce, stir to blend and cook as you would an omelette. Chop when cooked.
5 Add rice gradually to frypan ingredients, stirring through.
6 Add the egg and fold through.
7 Add salt and pepper.
8 Serve piping hot, or cold the next day!

Mexican Rice

Small Fibrous/Large Starchy Carbohydrate
45 minutes to make
Serves 4 adults

Ingredients

1 cup fat free chicken stock
1 small onion, chopped
1 small green capsicum, chopped
2 cups cooked white or brown rice
½ cup corn kernels
½ cup diced tomato
1 cup mild salsa (no oil)

Method

1 Using a large non-stick frypan on a medium heat, heat half the stock.
2 Add onion and capsicum and cook until tender.
3 Add corn, tomato, remaining stock and salsa.
4 Cook until boiling.
5 Stir in cooked rice, cover with lid, turn off heat and leave sitting for 5 minutes.
6 Great served as a side dish with fish or chicken.

Rice on the Side

B L D

Small Fibrous/Large Starchy Carbohydrate
40 minutes to make
Serves 4

Ingredients

250 grams brown rice
1½ cups corn kernels, cooked
2 eggs, beaten
1 small onion, finely chopped
soy sauce to taste
pepper to taste

Method

1 Cook rice until soft, then drain and wash well.
2 Into a large serving dish add the rice, mixed with corn.
3 In a small non-stick pan cook the eggs scrambled style, stirring all the time.
4 Add the onion to the egg and mix well.
5 Add the egg and onion to the rice and corn.
6 Pour a little soy sauce and pepper over the mixture and serve either hot or cold.

Japanese Rice (Chirashi Zushi)

B L D

Medium Protein/Medium Starchy/ Medium Fibrous Carbohydrate

30 minutes to make
Serves 4

Ingredients

375 grams short-grain white rice
3 cups water
1 small cucumber
1 teaspoon salt
6 teaspoons white vinegar (or rice wine)
3½ teaspoons sugar
100 grams white fish fillet
2 eggs, well beaten
90 grams peas, cooked
1 tablespoon shredded preserved ginger
Sauce:
2 tablespoons soy sauce
1 tablespoon white vinegar

Method

1 Wash rice, put into a heavy-based saucepan, cover with water and cook, covered, on low heat until tender. Put aside.

2 Wipe cucumber and rub with a little salt. Shred or grate, then marinate in a mixture of 3 teaspoons vinegar and 1 teaspoon sugar.

3 Steam or boil fish fillet until soft, then flake or chop coarsely. Sprinkle with a mixture of 3 teaspoons vinegar, 1½ teaspoons sugar and ½ teaspoon salt.

4 Mix eggs with 1 teaspoon sugar and $\frac{1}{2}$ teaspoon salt and pour into large non-stick pan. Cook until firm, turn and cook other side, then remove and cook.

5 When cool, shred with a sharp knife.

6 For the sauce, mix soy sauce with vinegar and pour into rice and mix in with a chopstick, then fold in fish, cucumber, shredded egg and peas.

7 Garnish with shredded ginger.

Rice Pudding

B L D

Large Starchy Carbohydrate
45 minutes to make
Serves 4 adults

Ingredients

250 grams white or brown rice
500 mL skim milk
2 dessertspoons 100% fruit jam of your choice
½ cup sultanas or raisins (or mixed)
½ teaspoon nutmeg
2 teaspoons vanilla essence
2 slices toasted white bread

Method

1 Preheat the oven at 205°C (400°F).
2 Place the rice, milk, fruit, nutmeg and vanilla essence in a casserole dish.
3 Spread the jam over the bread and cut into bite-sized squares.
4 Place pieces of bread over the top of the mixture so it fits like a lid.
5 Bake in the oven until brown and rice is cooked and thickened, approximately 40 minutes.

Desserts

Chocoholic's Dream

Berry Delight

Banana Split

Honey and Lemon Crêpes

Grapefruit Jelly Halves

B L D

Chocoholic's Dream

Small Protein/Medium Simple Carbohydrate
10 minutes to make
Serves 4 adults

Ingredients

1 L fat free chocolate ice-cream
600 mL low-fat vanilla custard
4 teaspoons low-fat chocolate topping
fat free chocolate powder (drink mix)

Method

1 This dessert is best served in either a tall, clear, dessert balloon or a clear bowl.
2 Spoon in the ice-cream, then layer in the custard, then topping. Repeat until the bowl is full.
3 Sprinkle generously with chocolate powder.

Berry Delight

Small Protein/Medium Simple Carbohydrate
10 minutes to make
Serves 4 adults

Ingredients

600 mL low-fat vanilla custard
4 dessertspoons fat free chocolate powder (drink mix)
1 L 99% fat free frozen fruit ice-cream
fresh mint for garnish
½ kilo fresh mixed berries (or any one alone)

Method

1 This dessert is best served in either a tall clear dessert balloon or a clear bowl.
2 First pour in the custard, evenly distributing it over the four dishes or glasses.
3 Sprinkle 1 dessertspoon of chocolate powder over each serving.
4 Tumble in the mixed or single berries, ensuring you fill the dish amply. Do not mix in with the custard.
5 Serve with some frozen fruit ice-cream and garnish with a sprig of fresh mint and a large strawberry split to sit on the side of the glass.

Banana Split   B   L   D

Small Protein/Medium Starchy Carbohydrate
10 minutes to make
Serves 4 adults

Ingredients

4 large ripe bananas
600 mL low-fat vanilla custard
400 mL low-fat natural yoghurt
4 dessertspoons honey
2 dessertspoons raisins

Method

1 Peel then slice the bananas down the centre and place in 4 suitable dishes.
2 Pour the desired amount of yoghurt and custard over them in a messy fashion.
3 Dribble honey over the dish and toss in raisins.
4 Serve with a cup of fat free hot chocolate made with skim milk.

Honey and Lemon Crêpes

B   L   D

Medium Starchy Carbohydrate
20 minutes to make
Serves 4–6 adults

Ingredients

2 cups plain flour
4 cups skim milk
2 eggs
2 cups fresh seasonal fruit, roughly chopped
2 lemons
honey

Method

1 Mix flour, milk and eggs in a bowl until light and airy.
2 In a very hot non-stick pan, pour in enough mixture to form a crêpe the size of a side plate.
3 When air bubbles appear on top of the crêpe and moisture has evaporated, carefully turn crêpe over.
4 After 30 seconds or so, slide crêpe out onto large plate.
5 Place fresh fruit into centre of crêpe, then roll into a loose tube.
6 Serve with honey and lemon.

Grapefruit Jelly Halves   B   L   D

Medium Fibrous Carbohydrate
20 minutes to make and overnight to set
Serves 4–6 adults

Ingredients

2 large, sweet-smelling grapefruit (yellow or pink)
1 packet low-calorie lemon jelly crystals
water as per the directions on jelly pack (less half a cup)
4 dessertspoons low-fat natural yoghurt *or* lemon sorbet yoghurt
4 sprigs fresh mint

Method

1 Wash grapefruit and slice in half. Empty the pulp, deseed, cut into cubes, and place into a mixing bowl. Be careful not to damage the outer skin halves.
2 In a separate bowl, mix the jelly crystals and water (less half a cup), as per the directions on the pack.
3 When jelly mix is thoroughly dissolved, add the grapefruit pulp, mixing well.
4 Place the grapefruit-skin halves in suitable bowls, and place in the refrigerator.
5 When the jelly has set, spoon into the skin halves and return to the refrigerator until ready to be served.
6 Serve with a dessertspoon of low-fat yoghurt and a sprig of fresh mint.

Snacks

Savoury Pancakes

Honey and Banana Pikelets

Country Scones

Strawberry, Guava and Banana Toast

Blueberry Protein Cakes

Savoury Pancakes

B   L   D

Small Protein/Medium Starchy Carbohydrate
20 minutes to make
Serves 2 adults

Ingredients

2 large washed potatoes
1½ cups self-raising flour
1 cup skim milk
2 eggs
4 large spring onions, finely chopped
handful of fresh parsley, finely chopped
1 teaspoon fat free vegetable stock powder
salt and pepper to taste

Method

1 Grate the potatoes, leaving the skin on.
2 In a large bowl, thoroughly mix all the ingredients, adding the milk a little at a time. Ensure that the consistency is fairly thick.
3 Heat a medium-sized non-stick frypan, making sure it is very hot before you begin to cook.
4 Spoon the mixture into the pan, creating pancakes approximately 10–15 cm in diameter.
5 When one side has browned well, turn and brown the other side. Make sure the middle is cooked right through.
6 Serve with eggs and a sprinkle of fresh parsley and a little salt, for breakfast at any time of the day (not night).
Note The mixture will spoil quickly, so make sure you cook it straightaway.

Honey and Banana Pikelets

B   L   D

Medium Starchy Carbohydrate
20 minutes to make
Serves 2 adults

Ingredients

1 medium-sized banana
2 eggs
2 tablespoons honey
1½ cups self-raising flour
1–2 cups skim milk
pinch nutmeg
fresh fruit and fruit jams for topping

Method

1 In a small bowl, mash the banana with the eggs and honey.
2 Together in a large bowl, mix all the ingredients well, adding the milk a little at a time. Ensure the consistency remains medium to thick. Try to froth the mixture slightly if possible.
3 Heat a medium-sized non-stick frypan, making sure it is very hot before you begin to cook.
4 Spoon the mixture into the pan to form pikelets approximately 5–10 cm in diameter.
5 When one side has browned well, turn and brown the other side. Make sure the middle is cooked right through.
6 Serve with 100% fruit jams and fresh fruit.

Country Scones

B L D

Medium Starchy Carbohydrate
10 minutes to make
Serves 4 adults

Ingredients

225 grams self-raising flour
pinch of salt
1 egg
150 mL skim milk
a little extra flour
100% fruit jams for topping

Method

1 Preheat the oven to 220°C (425°F).
2 Sift the flour into a large mixing bowl with the salt.
3 In a separate small bowl, whisk the egg.
4 Slowly pour egg into flour mixture, and rub with hands.
5 Knead the mixure to a soft dough, adding a little more milk if it feels at all dry. Be careful not to overhandle.
6 Roll in flour, keeping centre fairly moist. Flatten out until mixture is around 2½ cm thick. Cut into circles using a cutter or the top of a drinking glass.
7 Dust a non-stick baking tray with a little flour.
8 Set the scones around 3 cm apart.
9 Cook for 12–15 minutes, or until they have risen and are just golden brown.
10 Cool on a wire rack and eat slightly warm with some 100% fruit jam.

Strawberry, Guava and Banana Toast

Medium Starchy Carbohydrate
5 minutes to make
Serves 2 adults

Ingredients

4 slices heavily grained wholemeal and barley bread
strawberry and guava 100% fruit jam
1 banana

Method

1 Toast the bread until golden brown.
2 Spoon the required amount of jam on top.
3 Neatly slice the banana over the jam.
4 Serve hot with tea or coffee.

Blueberry Protein Cakes

B L D

Medium Protein/Small Starchy Carbohydrate
15 minutes to make
Serves 4 adults

Ingredients

1 punnet fresh blueberries
1 cup whey protein concentrate
1 cup self-raising flour
1 egg
1 cup milk

Method

1 In a small non-stick saucepan, lightly simmer the blueberries until soft.
2 Combine all ingredients in a large mixing bowl. The mixture should be of a pancake-like consistency.
3 Preheat a large non-stick frypan.
4 Spoon in the mixture, four at a time. Be careful to flip them over before they burn.
5 When the other side has almost cooked through, remove quickly from the pan.
6 Serve straightaway. These go stale after half a day, so only make what you need.

Party
Appetisers

Garlic King Prawns

Cold Dip Platter

San Choy Bow

Pizzettas with Sun-dried Tomatoes

Salmon and Potato Croquettes

B   L   D

Garlic King Prawns

Medium Protein
10 minutes to make
Serves 4 adults

Ingredients

½ cup fat free chicken stock
4 teaspoons crushed garlic
1 teaspoon finely chopped parsley
1 teaspoon salt
40 large, fresh, uncooked king prawns, peeled and deveined
½ cup white wine
1 lemon
pepper to taste

Method

1 In a large non-stick frypan, heat the stock, garlic, parsley and salt.
2 When the mixture is very hot, add the prawns and white wine, stirring constantly.
3 The prawns will be cooked in just a few minutes. They need to be served immediately with their sauce in a preheated dish with a wedge of lemon.

B   L   D

Cold Dip Platter

Large Fibrous Carbohydrate
10 minutes to make
Serves at least 4 adults

Ingredients

2 medium-sized carrots
2 celery stalks
8 medium-sized mushrooms
$1/2$ red capsicum
$1/2$ green capsicum
1 cup yellow squash
2 small tomatoes
handful of fresh snow peas
1 cup salsa (no oil)
$3/4$ cup low-fat ricotta cheese
$3/4$ cup sweet mustard pickles
1 cup apple sauce (no sugar added)

Method

1 Wash all the vegetables and slice into finger-sized pieces.
2 Using a large, open platter, arrange the vegetables into their own section.
3 In the middle, place three small bowls containing the salsa, ricotta cheese mixed with sweet mustard pickles, and apple sauce.
4 Serve chilled and fresh.

B   L   D

San Choy Bow

Medium Protein/Medium Fibrous Carbohydrate
20 minutes to make
Serves 4 adults

Ingredients

250 grams very lean beef mince
1 small onion, diced
1 teaspoon garlic salt
1 cup small broccoli heads
1 cup small cauliflower heads
1 small carrot, shredded
½ cup cabbage, shredded
1 teaspoon Chinese spices
pepper to taste
4 large, crisp, iceberg lettuce leaves

Method

1 In a hot, medium-sized non-stick frypan, toss the beef, onion and garlic salt.
2 When cooked, add all the vegetables except the lettuce, and cover with a lid. Cook until vegetables are only just soft (should still be very firm).
3 Trim the large lettuce leaves so they resemble the shape of a bowl.
4 Spoon the warm mince mixture into the cold lettuce leaves, sprinkle with pepper, and serve immediately.

Pizzettas with Sun-dried Tomatoes   B   L   D

Small Fibrous/Medium Starchy Carbohydrate
15 minutes to make
Serves 4 adults

Ingredients

1 long French breadstick, cut into 12 pieces
100 grams sun-dried tomatoes (not in oil), chopped
fresh basil
200 grams tomato purée
balsamic vinegar
salt and pepper to taste

Method

1 This recipe is really easy. Spread each slice of the French stick with tomato purée.
2 Sprinkle with a little fresh basil.
3 Top with some chopped sun-dried tomatoes.
4 Drizzle with a little balsamic vinegar and top with salt and pepper.
5 Grill until the sides of the pizzettas are golden brown and serve immediately.

B L D

Salmon and Potato Croquettes

Medium Protein/Medium Starchy Carbohydrate
25 minutes to make
Serves 4 adults

Ingredients

little skim milk
3 medium large washed potatoes
425 grams salmon (as little oil as possible)
1 egg
1 large onion, finely chopped
1 teaspoon fat free chicken stock powder
2 large spring onion stalks, finely chopped
2 teaspoons pepper
$^1\!/_2$ teaspoon salt
3 tablespoons cornflour (a little extra if necessary)
1 tablespoon water
1 lemon

Method

1 Boil potatoes in water with skin on. When cooked, mash with a little skim milk and put in mixing bowl.
2 Mix salmon, potatoes and remaining ingredients.
3 Take large dessertspoons of mixture and roll in your hands in a croquette shape. Roll it in a little cornflour on a sheet of wax paper. Add enough cornflour so mixture is not too wet.
4 Place the salmon croquettes in a preheated non-stick pan.
5 When they have browned slightly on one side, turn them over, add a tablespoon of water and place a lid on the pan.
6 Watch the croquettes carefully. When they have browned, turn off the heat.
7 Serve hot or cold with a crisp salad and a wedge of lemon.

fat free
forever
cookbook

Dianne Barker

More great recipes
– out now!

The *Fat Free Forever Cookbook* features over 100 mouth-watering fat free recipes. Enjoy curry laksa, fillet of beef with whole green peppercorns on potato mash, roasted Mediterranean vegetables, fragrant Thai prawns, Italian roasted pork with Roma tomato sauce, risottos and luscious desserts to tempt your palate and imagination. Enjoy eating all the foods you want to without the guilt! All these recipes are fat free (no added fat) and fit into the *Fat Free Forever! body shaping lifestyle*.

101 TIPS FOR WEIGHT LOSS

fat free forever tips

The Body
Shaping
Mini
Manual

Dianne Barker

Fat Free Forever Tips is an inspirational and practical companion to the *Fat Free Forever! body shaping lifestyle.*

Fat Free Forever Tips will motivate you to change the way you think and the way you eat and exercise. This book will help you lose weight and keep it off.

Testimonials

your say...

I want YOU
to contact me...

FEEDBACK!

I would like to thank the people who have read my book and taken the time to write about the wonderful changes they've experienced (see the following pages). I love getting these letters and want to encourage you to write, fax or email your comments about how *Fat Free Forever!* has helped change your life.

PHOTOS!

If you have any 'before and after' photographs, please send these to me also.

I wrote this book for you and it's important to me that what I'm saying is encouraging, applicable, and that it works (*and I know it does!*), so please feel free to contact me and let me know how you're going.

Dianne Wilson
Harry M. Miller & Co Management Pty Ltd
Level 4
171 William St
Darlinghurst NSW 2010
Ph: (02) 9356 0000
Fax: (02) 9356 0066
Email: linda@harrymmiller.com

For lecture and seminar bookings, please contact the above.

Dear Dianne

Just a note to say thank you for Fat Free Forever!
*I'm thrilled to say that your eating plan has worked
absolute wonders for me. I know I'm not supposed to
be weighing myself all the time, but there is now 13
kilograms less of me than at last November's
seminar! Very exciting and so easy! I remember being
very discouraged ... on the day of the seminar — I was
90.2 kilograms — I looked and felt incredibly fat.
(I'm thirty-seven years old, but for my first twenty-six
years, I looked like a stick. Ate whatever I fancied.
Then came the beginnings of middle-age spread ...
I thought that the spare tyre was there to stay!)*

*I started your plan the day after the seminar, following
just what I recalled of your session ... I've never eaten
so much (quality) food in my life, yet the first 2
kilograms literally fell off in the first week. That was
encouraging. I weaned myself from full cream to Lite
White milk by topping up the old container every time
I used some up. Breakfast is huge! And thank God for
those 'fat free' yoghurts.*

*After nine weeks (including a huge Junk Day at
Christmas and all those munchies at New Year), I'd
lost a total of 7 kilograms. The next 3 kilograms went
rather slowly, then it all levelled out. About this time,
a local health club slipped a card under my door.
(I don't have a car, so I get in plenty of walking; gyms
aren't me.) However, the card had one of those*

height/weight charts; I worked out I should have been 77 kilograms for my frame and height. I was very, very happy at 80 kilograms, but could I lose that last 3 kilograms?

Then your book came out! With the wonderful cornucopia of recipes within, the remaining weight was gone in a fortnight. I now have two Junk Days per week. My weight is still a steady 77 kilograms ...

By the way, a friend recently passed a kidney stone. [Using your book] he has lost 12 kilograms [in ten weeks] and his doctor is flabbergasted. His triglyceride and cholesterol counts are within normal parameters already. He'd been told it would take three years.

Ian McLean, NSW

Dear Dianne

Never before have I written to an author! I just had to on this occasion. I'm a self-confessed diet/health/fitness fanatic. I understand a lot about my body and how it works. Well, I thought I did.

I have just finished reading Fat Free Forever! *for the second time in two days. Today I started on the 'system'. I guess I should have waited until I showed a result to write and thank you, but I know I will show a result, so I'm writing to say congratulations in advance.*

It's common sense! It's easy!

I work out twice a day... over one-and-a-half hours a day. I eat fat free. I have plateaued. Nothing would kick-start me. My problem area is my tummy and I'm desperate to get rid of it. At thirty-seven and after two Caesareans I know it won't be perfect, but I want it better than it is and I believe I will have it.

I saw your book ... and it immediately excited and inspired me, not only to change my eating habits but to source out another gym and have them design a new program for me. Time is something I don't have (like everyone else), so it's really important to get it all right.

Thank you! This makes more sense than anything I've read. I'm going to buy a copy for my mum (who's overweight) and I've been recommending it to all who'll listen — yes! even before the result! It can't fail!

Denise Friend, NSW

Dear Dianne

I've just finished reading your book Fat Free Forever! *It was great, you did a great job, it's easy to understand and it makes sense...*
I am 39 years old, 163 centimetres tall and started off weighing 85 kilograms. I lost 4 kilograms while on holiday a few weeks ago when I started your program.

Annette Vidic, South Australia

Dear Dianne

I purchased your book Fat Free Forever! *after seeing you on the Bert Newton Show. I have been following the diet and think it's excellent!*

Nella Gerick, Victoria

Dear Dianne

I just wanted to say that I really loved the book you wrote. Thank you very much for it. I have always been obsessed about my weight. I used to always think I was too fat and I started going on diets and not eating at all.
My friends have read your book too and they loved it as well. It's working and I can notice it. Thanks again, and next time I'm in Australia I hope to meet you.

Sonja Dissanayeke, Sri Lanka, aged 16

PHOTO ACKNOWLEDGMENTS

Front cover photo: Nicole Anderson
Hair: Baci Hair Design
Swimwear: Sue Rice Swimwear

Photo of Dianne and family from *Back in Shape after Baby* by Dianne Wilson.
Courtesy HarperCollins Publishers.
Photographer: Femia Shirtliff

Photo of Bentley and Beau courtesy HarperCollins Publishers.
Photographer: Femia Shirtliff